OVERLOAD
The New Human Condition

LEOPOLD BELLAK, M.D.

HUMAN SCIENCES PRESS

A division of Behavioral Publications, Inc.

NEW YORK

Library of Congress Catalog Number 74-19052

ISBN: 0-87705-245-X

Copyright © 1975 by C.P.S., Inc., Box 83, Larchmont, New York

Published by Human Sciences Press, a division of Behavioral Publications, Inc., 72 Fifth Avenue, New York, New York 10011

Printed in the United States of America
5 6 7 8 9   9 8 7 6 5 4 3 2 1

Library of Congress Cataloging in Publication Data

Bellak, Leopold, 1916–
   Overload: the new human condition.

   Bibliography:　p.
   Includes index.
   1.　Social history—1945　　2.　Social problems.　3.　Social psychiatry.　I.　Title. HN18.B455　　362'.042　　74-19052

Contents

3

ACKNOWLEDGMENT

Ann Noll and Kenneth Nesdale are two of a sizable group to whom I am especially indebted for help with this volume.

L. B.

Preface

This book is an attempt to merge the clinical and research aspects of psychiatry into a unified method of assessing and perhaps influencing in some small way the critical condition of contemporary society. For some decades I have been professionally involved in crisis intervention among individuals, and in the last six years, the comparative study of adaptive ability among schizophrenic, neurotic and normal people has been the focus of my research.* By fusing these two approaches, it is my aim to offer a systematic assessment of some of the vast problems now faced by all of us—on the assumption that understanding is basic to change.

*This research, which was supported by a grant from the NIMH, is described in L. Bellak, M. Hurvich, and H. K. Gediman, *Ego Functions in Schizophrenics, Neurotics and Normals.* New York: John Wiley & Sons, 1973.

In that sense I hope this book can serve as a practical guide for individuals, committees and political leaders in their efforts to appraise and remedy social problems. The perpetual monitoring and "taking stock" of society that it facilitates will hopefully permit such preventive intervention as may some day stave off disaster.

At the heart of this approach is the concept of overload. This is a condition caused by an excessive number of often conflicting stimuli, which ceaselessly bombard an individual—or society—that is already strained to the breaking point. Given the obvious overload that is afflicting our society, some sort of intervention is required.

While the nature of specific problems will always vary, the underlying concept of overload will remain valid, and the resultant need for assessment and control will, in all probability, only grow more desperate. Today, for instance, the "future shock" that Toffler envisaged as a result of continued rapid technological development is probably less of an immediate danger than the world economic situation. Instead of being psychically overwhelmed by technology, we are faced with such concerns as lack of economic expansion, unemployment, depletion of natural resources, pollution, overpopulation and famine. As this book goes to press, the specter of the Great Depression of 1929 is more of a threat than brave new worlds of discovery.

It is present, not future shock we must deal with. Confusing signals overload us from all sides. Depression and inflation, in a combination new even to seasoned economists, are threatening the economy with collapse, and the resignation of former President Nixon has brought about a blow to credibility unequalled in memory.

The nature of problems change. The need to adapt to tremendous numbers of them persists. The scheme of assessment and intervention discussed here may be useful, regardless of what specific problems may afflict us at any particular time. Let me hope that I am right.

L. B.

chapter 1

OVERLOAD

In a controlled experiment, a guinea pig has learned to move in response to a bell to a location where it has come to expect food. When the experimenter rings the bell and then, when the animal is on its way to the accustomed location for food, administers an electric shock, it will hustle back to its corner. As it gets hungrier, the guinea pig will again venture forth in response to the bell, and this time gets the food without the shock. This apparently random process continues; sometimes the guinea pig receives a shock when he goes for food, and sometimes he receives none. The animal soon begins to shuttle back and forth between its corner and the point at which it gets the shock. Hunger drives it on, and uncertain fear drives it back. In its uncertainty, the guinea pig will finally sit down somewhere and gnaw its feet in dejection and agitation. The previously learned adaptive response to the bell as a signal

for food does not work any longer. The unsure animal suffers from an adaptive crisis.

The guinea pig is lucky: it has run into only a few
confusing stimuli. The rest of us are overloaded by a
barrage of many more complex and contradictory
signals.

The confusing impact of media, politics, travel,
science and the population explosion is bringing contemporary man dangerously close to a similar state of
disorganization—the state typically described as a
"nervous breakdown." We behave like people
caught on a merry-go-round that is spinning too fast
—as we reach for the brass ring that continually
eludes our grasp.

What has us spinning is the tremendous overloading of our senses, our intellect, our emotions.
Ours is a world that makes us dizzy with constant
changes. Above all, we are hit with *too much, too
fast.* Like the guinea pig's, our signals are conflicting;
what is worse, there are too many of them, and they
are constantly changing.

Overload is a term commonly used in relation to
electrical circuitry. If you have the refrigerator, the
washing machine and the air conditioner going simultaneously, and then turn on the electric oven as
well, your electrical system might well be overloaded. Fuses may blow, circuit breakers disconnect;
current may be cut off completely.

The brain is a complex system of electric circuitry, which, when overly bombarded with stimuli,
can, in effect, short circuit. Under ideal circumstances, synaptic connections are re-established and
realign to handle the load with efficiency beyond the

capability of mere electrical wiring. But if the conditions are less than ideal, much more severe and permanent damage can occur.

Much of the overload in our daily life is so well known that it does not even bear mentioning. On any given day, the radio, television or newspaper will enumerate a dozen crises taking place at that moment in various corners of the world.

What may not be quite so obvious is the crisis that can result from an overload of conflicting information. Take, for example, these two people sitting in a small restaurant about to order lunch:

"Better not beef, it's high in cholesterol," says one to the other. "Why not have the fish?"

"But the fish is probably full of mercury."

"And the crabs are high in cholesterol, pollution and mercury."

"Well, the vegetables will save us."

"You mean with their high concentration of pesticides?"

Perhaps they were half joking, but they were afflicted nonetheless with a very real case of overload. Such a huge quantity of conflicting information makes sorting it all out a major task. Even scientists are having trouble keeping up with and evaluating all the research being done. The food conversation above could easily go on indefinitely, but eventually the two diners would probably end up like the guinea pig: dazed, resigned, and unable to act.

Suppose the conversation continues:

"Who cares about cholesterol? Either you are going to get a coronary or you're not; it all depends on your personality."

"As a matter of fact," someone at a neighboring table chimes in, "if you have a family history, you're in for it."

"Not so. If you avoid too much cholesterol from the start, it really makes a difference. But once you're 35, the cholesterol's already there, and it's too late for a change in diet to do any good."

This was a restaurant close to a hospital, with a lot of medical clientele, all of whom were stuck in the same situation: they had a lot of information, and no way of evaluating it. But medical overload is matched by political and economic overload; our precariously balanced system must cope with such unpredictable factors as starvation in India, Arab oil, and the price of gold.

What we need is the ability to adapt. This requires first a careful scanning of all the data charging in on us. Then we need an analysis of how we are being affected, and finally how we need to behave in order to control its effect. After all this has been done, we may be able to survive our current catastrophic condition of constantly threatening overload.

Illness and health are, to a large extent, a matter of adaptation, and many an adaptive process has its crisis. Before penicillin more or less overcame pneumonia, textbooks spoke of passing through a crisis followed by a lysis. This was a correct and dramatic way of seeing the struggle of adaption, in this case between the pneumococcus and the patient. In many diseases the battle between the invading organisms and the human leads to a crisis—the acute illness. This is followed by an adaptation which involves a destruction of most invaders, an increased immunity of the human host against further illness that in turn may permit millions of these viruses or bacteria to live with impunity in this host.

Very frequently, unlike this case, the processes of adaptation are silent ones and not histrionic. Everybody's tonsils are quite normally inhabited by millions of bacteria. The human body and the bacteria have learned to adapt to each other in a way that generally causes neither of them much trouble. All that is needed, however, is to lower the bodily resistance of the human being, and one or the other of the always-present bacteria is likely to adapt to the new situation at the cost of the human host.

What has been said about physical illness holds true for mental illness and for mental balance. All our mental and emotional life involves a form of adaptation to the environment and to the forces within ourselves. Our aggressive and sexual drives, among others, are one force; our conscience and ideals of behavior and the rules and regulations and limitations of reality constitute another force. "Adjustment" means to be able to adapt one's own needs to the outside world. All of us quite normally go through maladaptive phases, and the only question is the degree of maladaptation and sometimes the length of the maladaptation. If the degree of adaptive failure is very marked, then we usually speak of mental illness, and, depending upon the severity of the adaptive failure, we have different names for it. In the field of psychiatry, one particular form of adaptive problem has in recent years been described as crisis adaptation, and the methods of dealing with it have been described as crisis intervention. The implication is that a relatively healthy person faces bigger problems than usual and is almost overtaxed by these problems. If the adaptation does not take too long and does not imply too severe a disruption of the normal processes, we do not yet call it an illness. Crisis adaptation can, however, turn into an illness of greater or lesser gravity.

Much depends on the individual's ability to exercise adaptive mechanisms in a healthy, temperate manner. Different people, of course, react differently to crisis as well as to other situations. Such diversity is equally apparent in the uses to which the individual's adaptive mechanisms are put in the face of changing social, economic, political and environmental conditions.

Most typologies suffer from oversimplification and overgeneralization, and, at best, constitute a model to which a number of people conform to a greater or lesser degree. Relatively pure types of reaction patterns, of personality, are rare, if they even exist at all. Yet, if used correctly, such descriptions of "type" are a useful way of indicating how a person will react in a crisis situation.

Our society of crisis has produced a certain type of character all its own, as we discuss later on in the chapter on object relations; mostly, it demonstrates a general tendency for people to have shallow relations with other people, with more people, over shorter periods of time. This holds true especially for the generation born since Hiroshima.

For the generation older than that, there are some well-known character types who react to the crisis we confront daily in certain relatively clearcut ways. The more uncertain our lives become, the more most of them seem to become pure types. The country seems to go through phases during which a majority—or at least a high percentage of those in pivotal positions—are dominated sometimes by one type, and sometimes by the other.

The eggheads and the squareheads are among the most interesting of these types. The *majority* of the people stay somewhere in the center, but it takes only a small percentage to swing a general election one way or the other. In that sense, one could say that the Kennedy era was one primarily of egghead characteristics, and Nixon's was dominated by squareheads. Either type, in moderation, is easy enough to live with, and no occasion for name-calling. Toward the more extreme fringes, some real social dangers exist.

An egghead, by and large, is a person who has, as an intellectual, a predilection for, and a preoccupation with, abstract issues. There is a tendency toward self-doubt, skepticism and inquiry, and at least a measure of what psychologists have called "tolerance for ambiguity."

Some people, however, need things always black and white. While it is true that people with little intelligence can only work concretely, some people with high IQ's can see things only in black and white because it is emotionally impossible for them to stand ambiguity. They may have a hard time tolerating shadings because they need to think of good and bad in absolute terms: they must be sure of staying on the good side. Rigid walls are their solution to any conflict. The eggheads are a constant threat to the squareheads because they threaten the black and white and good/bad foundation on which alone the latter can resolve a crisis.

Thanks to a number of social psychologists, one of the most outspoken forms of squarehead, the authoritarian personality, has been well described and can be clearly identified by such tools as psychological tests. The usual academic quibbling notwithstanding, the authoritarian personality is consistently shown to have a low tolerance of ambiguity and a variety of definite developmental and psychological characteristics.

One social psychologist, Rokeach, has spoken of the open and the closed mind, characterized by an open and a closed "belief system." I would characterize eggheads then as having relatively open, and squareheads as relatively closed, belief systems.

The "belief system" serves the squarehead as his guide to the world, to closeness or distance to people: he can be close to "good" people and distant to "bad" people. Naturally, "good" may mean different things in different subcultures: political, economic, racial, religious, occupational, and other values, but the squarehead knows only one kind—*his*. Such rigid belief systems were adopted by the Nazis, who were squareheads in the extreme, as well as by all varieties of religious, political, and racial bigots.

Religious systems, i.e., organized religion, can foster very firm belief systems. To the extent to which salvation is said to predicate on certain types of values, prayers, behavior and customs, everyone not part of that belief system tends to be seen as alien, potentially dangerous and inimical. That such a belief system may cause bloody divisions among people who are otherwise indistinguishable can be seen, for instance, in the violent strife between Catholics and Protestants in Northern Ireland. As children are imbued with religious belief systems at an early age, and the price of transgression or disbelief is very high (life versus death; heaven versus hell), these belief systems tend to be particularly strong, and, when not tempered by other considerations, tend to create squareheads.

Squareheads are made, not born. If a child is brought up restrictively, with strong punishment for any show of aggression, independence, or other drive, he is likely to become a squarehead: he will control his own aggression so well that he will feel he has none—except what is sanctioned by authority, in the service of authority, or the "good" side. Being tightlipped and tight sphinctered otherwise, he will become the guardian of other people's good behavior to control his own.

Squareheads are necessary in many ways, and good in certain crises. They are equipped with such highly developed defenses and structured belief systems that they meet without hesitation many crises that would disturb or confuse the egghead.

Eggheads rarely become generals or even policemen; these are occupations that require not only prompt action on the basis of simplified or codified strong convictions (eggheads can do that if they must), but also enough absolute certainty to preclude the prolonged self-questioning afterwards that destroys peace of mind.

An egghead, in distinction to the squarehead, has an attitude of reasonable doubt, including self-doubt, which includes, at least intermittently, an ability to see more than one side. Eggheadedness can, of course, be overdone, and lead to incapacitating doubt and inability to act.

The willingness to laugh at oneself, and at human foibles in general, is characteristic of the egghead. While squareheads are generally sober men who take themselves quite seriously, their counterparts have the distance, tolerance of ambiguity and irreverence essential to a sense of humor.

Squareheads are often called realists. What this usually means is that they can see the immediate, concrete reality. This may also mean, however, that they are unable to see the reality around the corner. For that same reason, eggheads are often mistaken for dreamers because they are willing to forego some immediate goal for the sake of a larger though more distant one involving a good deal of "detour" thinking.

To the extent to which a political party implies a belief system, to that extent it may predispose the squareheads among each party to constitute a stereotype. But no particular party has a monopoly on squareheadedness. While it may be more obvious among reactionary types, there is no question that the so-called knee jerk liberal, though appearing to be an egghead, is a liberal squarehead—a closed mind on the liberal end of the spectrum. Communists, of course, tend to have a completely rigid outlook, their strong belief system assuming the role of a state religion.

The crisis in American life has led to polarization of all kinds, as individuals, disoriented by their rap-

idly changing environment, cling more and more
stubbornly to their particular beliefs and character
types. Belief systems have become not only more set
and more extreme, but also more deliberate as pro-
ponents attempt to gather their adherents and
solidify from among their own ranks. In the 1972
presidential election, Republicans around former
President Nixon became, by stated desire, more conservative, and Democrats around Senator McGovern
cultivated their liberalism.

The men surrounding Nixon in the White
House, apparently by their own admission, and even
preference, exemplified squareheadedness. An issue
of *Newsweek* featuring Haldeman on its cover described him as believing in discipline, hard work and
efficiency:

> Haldeman is Social Director: Haldeman, him-
> self very nearly monastic in the service of the
> President, has extended the purity of the faith
> down to who sees whom after hours. "He's like
> a Kremlin Commissar," says one nettled Re-
> publican. "The worst crime he can think of is
> cosmopolitanism."

Hopefully it is possible that in our ever-shrinking
world, where long-distance communication, media
and travel keep people everywhere in contact with
each other, it will become increasingly difficult to
breed the squarehead. Intelligent mental hygiene in
the upbringing of children could certainly serve as a
preventive measure.

As stated earlier, squareheads do not come from
nowhere. Their attitude is a logical outgrowth of cer-

tain needs, and represents one logical and moderately effective way of coping with overload. Their rigid belief system screens out confusing stimuli and molds what data does get through to fit a predetermined and manageable pattern.

There are other ways of reacting to overload, however. One reaction has been an attempt simply to leave; countless subcultures—hippies, beatniks, superintellectuals, drug enthusiasts and mystics—have all taken the route of spiritual exit.

A return to a more primitive lifestyle—as symbolized by communal farms and homebaked bread—was one response to crisis that came into prominence particularly in the late 1960s. Such ideas are not new; Thoreau and Rousseau before him are prime exponents of this attempt to deal with the complexities of our social relations by rejecting them entirely. Rousseau felt that the progress of the sciences contributed to the corruption of man. He believed that laws were a device of oppressors to maintain their grip. Then, as now, a feeling of being overwhelmed by the increasing complexity of science and our social structure was the mainspring of attempts to take the sting out of it by reverting to a more egalitarian, less hierarchical, simpler way of life.

Rousseau was the first of the romanticists, influencing many outstanding writers, social theorists, politicians, and educators as diverse as Goethe, Tolstoy, Robespierre and the famous Swiss educator, Pestalozzi. Yet it is not unreasonable to speak of his main propositions as the "Rousseau Delusion:" the persistent belief, largely held against evidence to the contrary, that we can turn the clock back socially, scientifically and technically in order to have a better life.

Surely the excesses of our civilization, the senseless arms race toward destruction, the keeping up with the Joneses, and the pretentions of the self-righteous make Rousseau and the cult of "dropping out" of society appealing alternatives. The trouble is that one extreme is apparently not the best answer to the other extreme.

The violence at Altamont and subsequent festivals, for example, indicates that the peace that prevailed at Woodstock may have been more a fortunate accident than a social prescription. It demonstrates, too, the particular vulnerability of the "Woodstock generation" to incursions from the very violence they have tried to escape.

The Rousseau Delusion is not limited to youth by any means. There are businessmen who become priests out of similar motives. There are other prime exponents of our competitive society who dream of changing to a simple life, and some even do it. There is the desire for a farm in even more people than those who can afford one to take refuge in on weekends: it is heartwarming, amusing, and heartbreaking to see highpowered executives, politicians, and other infighters revel in dirty dungarees and even dirtier feet on places as diverse as Martha's Vineyard, Fire Island, Bucks County, or Wyoming, proclaiming that this is the real life. There they feel they have washed off their pretenses, their voraciousness, and vicious maneuvers to stay alive and ahead of the other fellow. In solitude they lick their wounds from hand-to-hand combat.

It is too easy, though, to mistake form for substance. Open shirts and flowers are not sufficient to deal with the complexities of our world. They are a beginning. We may do away with some detour behavior, but most of it is indispensable. People who dream of getting away to the simple life suffer from the *delusion* that there is an attainable state of bliss; and to a certain extent, such a delusion is vital, an integral part of living. To join the Rousseau delusion to the one of an attainable state of bliss is likely to be ineffective and lead to disaster. It is the result of fear and a lack of a frame of reference.

What is essential is a careful re-examination of what we need to live in the world we made. In personal life as well as in international life there are no easy solutions, only detours, because ours is an intricate road with stop lights, bypasses, and other devices necessary not to crash into each other.

Rather than attempting to assess or deal with the problems of our contemporary crises in broad character types or oversimplified solutions, it behooves us to study society and contemporary man in crisis in clinical detail, as psychologists and psychiatrists and psychoanalysts study other problems of living.

Institutions, cultures and societies are systems of adaptation to the environment. The systems go through different phases of development and sometimes undergo crises in adaptation; and sometimes the systems of the society function so poorly that the society can be ill. In fact, some cultures and societies have malfunctioned to such an extent that they have disappeared from the face of the earth. The question of whether our contemporary society suffers primarily from a crisis or, rather, from an illness, will eventually be answered only when we know the outcome.

That is, the best psychiatric clinicians acknowledge the difficulty of deciding at times whether an adolescent is merely showing aggravated symptoms of adaptation to the many changes in his body, mind and social role, or whether he is indeed demonstrating the beginnings of a psychotic process.

Our society is in a state analogous to the state of a troubled adolescent.

It is often said that our world is becoming crazier all the time. If being crazy means having a hard time adapting to the world as it is (a definition that I agree with), then society *is* crazy. Our perplexity about the many new things around us and our shaky sense of security, threatened by today's rapid pace of change, result in a disorientation and inability to adapt comparable to schizophrenic behavior.

Secretary General Waldheim of the United Nations described the atmosphere well when he spoke, in September 1974, of the world being in a crisis of "helplessness." He referred to "an almost universal sense of apprehension" coupled with a sense of helplessness and fatalism, which he found deeply disturbing. And well he ought to, because the fatalism or apathy to which he referred is the final result of an inability to cope: the guinea pig who has failed to deal with the confusing stimuli and overload of different signals usually sits apathetically in a corner and chews its feet aimlessly.

Home used to make people feel safe. The standard worry of the innocent American tourist abroad was: is the water safe for drinking? Now, however, he must be periodically alerted to the dangers of pollution in his own air and drinking water, often the result of chemicals whose very existence was previously unknown to him.

Not only are we subjected to polluted water and food contaminated by pesticides and additives, but the air we breathe is heavily laden with lead from hightest gasolines, so that chronic low-level lead poisoning is frequent. When casein derivatives were first developed into plastic material, nobody dreamed of the pernicious contribution they would eventually make to our pollution problems.

A new threat to our health, even our survival—in fact, potentially one of the gravest discoveries in recent years—was revealed on the front page of the *New York Times* only weeks after Secretary General Waldheim's speech: the ozone in our atmosphere, which protects us from the deadly effects of ultraviolet radiation, is under attack from chemicals released into the air from aerosol cans.

Fluorocarbons, chemical compounds used as propellants in aerosol sprays, have been discovered to have a destructive effect on the ozone layer in the stratosphere which is essential to all forms of land life. The inert chemical does not react with the various deodorants, insecticides and hairsprays it propels; once expelled from the can, however, it drifts up into the stratosphere. There it absorbs ultraviolet light, releasing chlorine. This chlorine begins a chemical process that destroys the ozone.

The Harvard researchers who made the finding, Doctors Michael B. McElroy and Steven C. Wofsy, predict that even if the propellants were banned by 1980, the ozone could be depleted by 14 to 15 percent by the year 2000.

Scientists are uncertain what effects this ozone depletion would have. The minimum risk, some believe, will be an increase in the danger of skin cancer. Others fear changes in climate, with more heat finding its way through the reduced ozone layer into the lower atmosphere, where it could cause wind shifts and changes in the world's weather.

Technology poses other, equally fantastic threats to our lives. A proposal to divert the waters of the Yukon River in Alaska might spell disaster for all of us. If the project were carried out, it is suggested that the earth's surface waters would shift, possibly causing the tilt of the earth's axis to change. The potential consequences of such an occurrence are, to say the least, unimaginable.

It is not only the citizen on Main Street, U.S.A., who is exposed to these frightening experiences; what of the peasant in India who suddenly finds that his little piece of land will no longer grow his foodstuffs? The new irrigation system for the Ganges and Indus Rivers have caused the water table of the flat plains to rise, resulting in salt contamination of the topsoil. What of the Egyptian farmer who has been blessed with the Aswan Dam—only to find that the permanent, stable lake formed behind the dam is encouraging the growth of snails that infect humans with the virulent disease called schistosomiasis?

Threats to our freedom of movement, threats to our civil liberties and sometimes even threats to our lives confront us as never before.

• Bumper-to-bumper traffic prevents many people from traveling when and where they please, while deteriorating public transportation systems make getting to work an unpredictable nightmare.

• The CIA and the Army have compiled computer banks of information about citizens who have dissented on some issues.

• The Atomic Energy Commission alone decides what information on atomic energy—e.g., location of plants, method of commercial use—will be released to the general public.

• Skyjacking, virtually unheard of five years ago, became an accepted phenomenon as long as it was limited to brief, safe sorties to Havana. Recently, however, the lives of hundreds of innocent victims all over the globe have been endangered by sky-jackers, forcing the airlines to make interminable and undignified searches of all the passengers waiting to board the plane.

• Irrational bombings—on quiet streets, in office buildings, in department stores, on college campuses—are constant threats to our safety.

All of these pressures, events and threats lead to confusion, uncertainty and incredulity in the daily life of the average person. Some people become angry, some disgusted, others frightened. Many just want to get away from it all. From time immemorial man has hunted for a better place to live. The Paradise of the Greeks and Romans, the Valhalla of the Germanic warriors and the Judeo-Christian Garden of Eden are all variations of the utopia that man believes must exist somewhere. Sometimes the quest has been for more tangible bliss, as when, in antiquity, hordes of people drove southward toward the sun, or when the Huns pressed westward from the high plateaus of Asia in search of food.

This same aspiration for a more pleasurable state now drives many Americans abroad—to Spain, to England, to tropical lands—anywhere in an attempt to escape the hectic confusion of their world. It is not only the search for paradise and the desire to escape the turmoil of society, or even the expensive upkeep of houses and cars that sends Americans abroad. Many of them also hope to find a form of self-realization that is difficult to achieve here in the United States. We can only hope they succeed, though I am afraid that at best success would be only temporary. America is simply the vanguard of the entire world's increasingly advancing technology, its increasingly furious interaction between man and machine, private lives and public events. Although there are still places where the pace of life is fairly slow, as in Wyoming or in the South Pacific, chances are that there can be no permanent escape from twentieth-century society; there are only better ways of dealing with it. We cannot destroy the machines and we cannot turn the clock back. There is probably no real escape anywhere.

There are awesome, even frightening possibilities of new developments, almost limitless in logic and ingenuity, which man is forced to consider as he plunges on, gripped in his tiny genius by the Everest syndrome—climbing every technological summit just because it is there. Our society is full of constant changes, more drastic than ever before, that call for tremendous adaptation. We hardly have the opportunity to adjust to "the average expectable environment." We are forced to cope with an environment in which nothing stays the same for any appreciable length of time. We make too many technical advances too fast, and we get too much news to digest and make sense of. It all adds up to what is sometimes called an "informational overload."

In 1961 I published a paper in the *Archives of General Psychiatry* called "Personality Structure in a Changing World." It seemed to me even then that the problems in adaptation to change would lead to more superficial human relations; so much input from so many sources would force us to try to protect ourselves from emotional overload by putting up barriers against relationships that are too close:

> The outstanding characteristic of American culture today is the impact of communication and change: television, radio, newspapers, magazines, and tons of professional literature bombard us constantly. The loss of identity of modern man is largely the result, I believe, of adaptation to a constant flow of changing stimuli; any event, indeed any individual, is merely a matter of the moment. There can no longer be a Dreyfus affair or a Sacco and Vanzetti trial to stir the world for years; the most stirring events are immediately superseded by

other equally stirring events. . . . We can barely digest our breakfast news before more is in front of us. Add to this a tremendous social mobility—the fact that hardly anyone belongs to the socioeconomic group to which his parents, or even he himself, belonged some years ago— and one has a dizzy world of great achievements, great problems, and no fixed place to belong. Surely it is to be expected that people will tend to become alienated in such circumstances. There is no time for things, values, events, to become familiar, let alone deeply ingrained. In the past the process of adaptation, such as the attempts of nouveaux riche to adjust to their new status, was facilitated by the passage of time. Today, however, time only compounds the problem by presenting new difficulties that clamor to be dealt with and to which we must adapt.

chapter 2

Some Other
ADAPTATIONS to CRISIS
—Is Our Society Insane?

There are a good many similarities between the guinea pig we mentioned in the previous chapter, emotionally ill individuals and our unsure society today. Reasonably well-adjusted people at times become emotionally ill when major changes enter their lives. The death of a close friend or relative, the occurrence of a serious illness, a severe finanical loss can trigger this episode.

• Mary Jean Lewis had been considered a happy-go-lucky person who found a great deal of pleasure, not only in her everyday life as mother and wife, but also as a college professor. When her adolescent son died in an automobile accident she was understandably devastated. When weeks and then months went by, and she still refused to see old friends, or could not get herself to go to the butcher store where she had bought the steaks he had loved so much, and took no interest at all in her work, it was obvious that she suffered from more than the serious emotional crisis that would have been entirely normal. What made her depressive reaction a psychiatric illness rather than normal mourning was, among other things, the fact that she had really greatly identified with that son. She saw her aspirations potentially fulfilled in him. He was the boy she would have unconsciously liked to be. She had given him the love and admiration she had hoped to get from her own parents and had not. The tragic loss of this son for her was, in addition to the grief everyone would have felt, what we call a severe narcissistic blow. It thus affected her own self-esteem, her own goals, her conception of herself, to the point where it affected her vital functions.

• A number of people become emotionally ill during service in the Armed Forces because their ordinary daily routine has been replaced by a set of bewildering new circumstances. Tom Cook had been an outstanding student in high school, a great football player. He also did well in the sciences and was clearly top man on the campus in a small town. He could count on his measure of competence and respect. When he joined the Army, he was suddenly just one rookie among thousands. He was shuttled around, sworn at and felt completely anonymous. In his case, he became quite anxious and came to the attention of the psychiatrist. Originally, his self-esteem had not been very good. At home he had not felt much appreciated or sure of himself. His father had been an alcoholic and his mother had turned her interests everywhere but toward her children. With the help of his intelligence and athletic ability, he had adaptively repaired the poor image he had of himself by success in school. The Army restored a painful set of circumstances for him which caused his panic attacks as a failure of adaptation in comparison to many others.

• Gloria Smith, a small-town girl who joined the WACS, was suddenly thrown into a panic by close proximity to hundreds of girls and by the precipitous temptations of being among hundreds of sexually experimenting soldiers. We know that, conversely, the "reentry" problem of returning to civilian life often has mindwrecking effects.

• A *society* can also become nervous, peculiar and mentally ill, and show serious problems of adaptation. Puerto Rico, for instance, has changed in a relatively few years from a mostly rural society to an increasingly urban, industrialized one. In the typical Puerto Rican village, a child could grow up feeling entirely protected within the surroundings of the whole village. Many different people served maternal and paternal functions for him, and within the relatively unstressful setting, it was pleasant and easy to adapt, to grow up. When that same boy had to leave the village, unlike previous generations, and take a job on a steamshovel in an unfamiliar setting, with people he did not know, he developed some emotional problems. His child, in turn, grew up not in a protective multifamily village arrangement, but rather on the fast-growing edges of a town in which he only rarely saw his father, and where competitive striving, having to adjust to many quickly changing personalities, left him much less secure and more prone to mental illness. The result has rather convincingly been demonstrated by A. B. Hollingshead, a sociologist at Yale, who showed that the incidence of psychosis in Puerto Rico increased significantly with the break-up of village structure.

In recent years, increasing attention has been paid to psychological crises and their resolution. Erich Lindemann in a pioneering study observed normal and pathological grief reactions in the relatives of the victims of the 1942 Coconut Grove fire in Boston that took over 400 lives. He found that some engaged in normal grieving and were able to adapt by doing the "work of mourning," an acknowledgment of their loss, sadness and slow emotional disengagement from their departed. Others showed either insufficient mourning or failed to really come to grips with their loss. They tried to make relatively light of it but showed serious maladjustment by not really getting over the loss, as expressed through work impairment, not being able to marry again and bodily ailments. Others were overwhelmed by grief and remained in a withdrawn state. The people who were able to adapt led normal healthy lives after a suitable time interval.

A crisis exists when the problem-solving capacity of a person is severely taxed by life stress. If a solution to the crisis is not found, a period of disorganization ensues, leading to paralysis of action, symptom formation or maladaptive behavior. Eventually adaptation of some kind is arrived at, although not necessarily one in the best interests of that individual or others. Identification of the precipitating stress, which an individual patient or society may not be aware of, is of critical importance. Basically, crisis intervention, which in some cases is also called emergency psychotherapy, is an attempt to contribute to the restoration of the equilibrium.

It is my opinion that what can be said of a person in crisis can be said of a society in crisis. Historians and sociologists have not hesitated to speak of nations, of cultures, in adaptive terms, although they may not always have been explicitly aware of it.

The phrase "decline and fall of the Roman Empire" implies an organismic process. The term "golden age," as the Golden Age of Pericles, or of Rome, refers to different phases of a developing society; phases that are similar to Erik Erikson's formulation, expounded in *Childhood and Society,* of the eight stages of development of an individual's lifecycle.

The Roman Empire in its heyday indicated adaptive aspects with regard to administrative roles. Creative potential and drive control, orderly delegation of executive duties and good object relations were a part of the well-functioning Empire. The decline was marked by lack of ability to deal with emergent problems, lack of frustration tolerance and a simplistic hedonistic outlook on life.

German society, before the advent of Hitler, can also best be characterized by its adaptive failures. A lowered self-esteem after a lost war played a predominant role. An upheaval in class structure led to maladaptive defense mechanisms such as feelings of alienation, perplexity and polarization. The primative Germanic superego, accustomed to external control, was not up to self-control. Erich Fromm rightly suggests in *Escape from Freedom* that such was the feeling of alarm about sudden freedom that the turn toward authoritarianism was a welcome flight from fear of loss of control. Albert Speer, Hitler's minister of defense, tells in his recently published diary that his mother was attracted by the "orderliness" of the Nazi storm troopers. To see them march in cadence was welcome to the people thrown into panic by the chaos of self-determination and the trial and error of the Weimar Republic.

Margaret Mead, in her 1935 book *Sex and Temperament in Three Primitive Societies,* describes the modes of adaptation of these societies as if they were individuals. Barbara Tuchman, the historian, in her book, *The Proud Tower,* examines the societies that engaged in World War I from the vantage point of adaptive failure, also much as one might describe individuals. The European nations, led by the Kaiser and the inept French and British leaders, blundered into adaptive failure, almost certainly without compelling need and out of their own inadequacies.

Surely the analogies that can be drawn between individuals and such conglomerates as nations and societies are severely limited. A group, being a configuration, is more than the sum of individuals. Some characteristics are bound to be submerged and new ones bound to be emergent. Special propositions hold true for the behavior of groups and nations that do not apply to the behavior of individuals. There are, nevertheless, enough behavioral and adaptive features common to both to enable us to study societal and national behavior using methods of individual appraisal.

The most striking feature of modern American society is its extreme mobility, both geographical and social. Certainly such flexibility increases personal freedom, but it also engenders changes that have a less happy effect on personal (and social) well being.

Hopeless attempts to adapt to a too-broad, too-rapidly changing world can result in superficiality at best and disorganization and maladaptation at worst. A headline from *The Wall Street Journal* points up some of the problems: "Growing job-demands shatter the marriages of more executives. When the firm comes first, wives grow bitter; most companies offer no help. . . ."

Rootlessness and a lack of deep relationships may become more and more bearable, but there is a limit to how far lack of commitment can safely take us. The modern notion of uninvolvement, when it is taken one step further, results in a pathological detachment from reality, i.e., modern society's mental illness.

Physical change and growth and confusion are, however, only a small part of the story of our society's ills. The constant shift in value systems is at least as confusing as technological change. A value feels like a value only when one has grown accustomed to it. In contemporary society, the constant shifting of values causes disorientation, even if the shifts are for the better. One feels alienated because things feel unfamiliar. Today's values must be elastic in order to stretch to accommodate the rapid changes of our social structure without breaking under the strain. When values become too fluid, however, we no longer perceive them as values. Our values seem so very accommodating that they change with every cultural shift. Since we do not have time to get used to them, it is not surprising that we find it hard to recognize them as values at all. A father who complains that his son does not appreciate the value of money must realize that money no longer holds the same value as it did when the father was younger. The last generation gave up independence of job choice for the security of pension plans and fringe benefits—benefits which, in varying degrees, lessen individualism. When the major focus in life shifts in one generation from spouse, family, home and breadwinning to "finding oneself" as an individual in a commune-type relationship as a multi-family with no material desires, we find a startling change in value systems.

The United States is not the only country to undergo these startling shifts in values. Since World War II, changes have also, for instance, affected the social values of Japan. Whereas in an earlier day self-sacrifice and tradition were the most respected values, now, the job turnover rate for men under the age of 20 is said to be about 30 percent annually, and the pursuit of pleasure has become accepted. Values have been turned on end for young Japanese born into a society stunned by military defeat and then reordered by a Western military occupation force.

Money in our culture is much more fluid now than it used to be. "Fly now, pay later" is an acceptable philosophy because there is more assurance that one will have money to pay "later" than there was 20 years ago. Keynesian deficit spending has become *the* mode of living. Many older people are understandably uneasy about it and are therefore in conflict with the younger generation. Steady inflation, which has eroded the dollar to about 50 percent of its value of some 20 years ago, further adds to the confusion. A man who earns $25,000 today and still clings to the vision of what it could buy 20 years ago is, quite simply, bewildered; its purchasing power, in fact, is only half of what it was in the early 1950's.

With the help of the mass media, changes in one place produce changes in other places; therefore the number of changes in any given place multiplies more rapidly than ever before. Cultural relativity means relative moral values, which provide less of a frame of reference than absolute standards. Constant shifting takes place in fashion, art and even in the role of age. What was once considered middle age is now young; by the age of fourteen, a person is now considered grown up. What is more, the word "generation" conveys a shorter and shorter time span. Anyone who comes in contact with college students has found that students no more than two years apart often regard one another as belonging to different "generations."

Such changes in values were never quite so rapid or drastic as they are today, but similar periods of major change have produced similar value upheavals in the past: the fall of the Roman Empire, the end of the Feudal Age, the Industrial Revolution, the First World War. Changing sexual mores are nothing new; they occur in every war and postwar era. England before Cromwell and England after were so different as to appear two different countries. The twenties in the United States, as typified by the lifestyle of Zelda and Scott Fitzgerald, and in Germany, as depicted in the musical *Cabaret*, were full of marked sexual changes—an emphatic reaction to the Victorian era of repressed sexual attitudes. Nevertheless, a point can be made that these changes are even more pronounced today and affect an infinitely larger part of the population than ever before. Medicine has been a big factor in spurring sexual changes. Penicillin, for example, removed the fear of syphilis and gonorrhea that had previously been a potent force in regulating sexual conduct. The Pill has played a tremendous role in altering sexual mores; the changed attitude toward abortion and illegitimate children is a far cry from the attitudes of the characters in Theodore Dreiser's *An American Tragedy*.

The American attitude toward sex has always been rather rigid compared to that in countries such as France, Japan and India. Americans now have more sexual freedom than they know what to do with and, as a result, often behave like smirking adolescents. People other than the very young are particularly caught in this change of values; they are unsure when to behave according to the new system and when according to the old. As a result, frequent behavior swings occur from one to the other.

Affluence has become a goal in itself rather than merely the product of hard work. Work lacks meaning. There is less pride in a job well done than ever before, partly as a result of socioeconomic changes and partly as a result of the move from self-satisfying handicrafting to industrial labor done for others. The trouble is that the human being seems to be the kind of animal whose inner self-esteem and happiness depend on the relatively stable value of doing work for its own sake. *Ars gratis artis.* Art is its own reward. When personal achievement is only a means to an end (such as money or fame), rather than a satisfying end in itself, a certain feeling of emptiness is bound to ensue. The "outer directedness" sociologist David Riesman has spoken of in *The Lonely Crowd* largely results from the pressures imposed by a modern, mass-producing society in which man becomes an entirely public rather than a private person. He must relinquish traditional values in order to "get along." Put in its simplest terms, people have had to learn to conform to others to such an extent that they can scarcely afford to acknowledge even their own instincts. Riesman calls it "catering to group needs."

The value of competence, though internal, had its external roots in the fact that a favorable reputation was vital for one's job security. In a society of abundance and fast mobility, competence is even more necessary and less possible, and hardly anyone remains well known long enough to accrue benefits from a good reputation. Status has become even less stable than previously because of the socioeconomic mobility of our society. Those who attain signal successes are soon crowded out by new celebrities and forgotten.

In pre-World War Europe, status was clearly indicated; aristocratic titles as well as business titles, such as *Kommerzialrat,* were an important part of the language. Eminent men were well known even in major cities. If a Viennese behaved peculiarly in a streetcar, the streetcar conductor was as likely as not to say, "If you don't stop behaving that way, I will send you to Wagner-Jaurreg." The then professor of psychiatry at the University of Vienna was well enough known to most Viennese that mentioning his name was the New York equivalent of saying, "I'll send you to Bellevue."

There is no parallel to this type of established status in most of American culture, with the exception perhaps of some Southern towns and some small country towns. In the relatively status-free society of the United States, the search for a clearly established social position once upon a time led some Americans to engage in the exercise of marrying titled Europeans. Status in this country is still determined to a certain extent by the size of one's income, what one wears, where one lives and shops and the country club one belongs to. But the marked redistribution of wealth begun during the New Deal period has helped blur class distinctions. The upper, middle and lower class framework and the values defined by each level are rapidly disappearing. (One striking example of this is the changing admissions policies of colleges. More doors are now open to minority groups, and the sons of the Establishment must now compete with them on sheer academic merit.)

Widespread alienation and dissolution of time-honored values have understandably increased uncertainty in our society. A society, like an individual, becomes frightened when it is unsure. Fear leads to irrationality and irrationality to destructive behavior. Increasingly, our current crises are causing some people to compare our society with that of the Weimar Republic—the government that was superseded by the rise of Hitler. Walter Laqueur, Director of the Institute of Contemporary History and Wiener Library in London, enumerated the following similarities: in Germany, as in contemporary society, youth became nihilistic; intellectuals mostly lost faith and contact with what was going on; obscure art forms, addiction to drugs, perversions and sexual promiscuity blossomed; the old aristocracy and military castes were out but nothing new had as yet been able to fill the void.

While Laqueur points out that the similarities between Germany in the Nazi era and America today are important to keep in mind, he also calls attention to the differences between the two societies. For example, the Germans had just been defeated in World War I and the country had lost much of its territory. Further, Germany had had no experience with democracy. And there was a major economic crisis and widespread poverty and uncertainty. Still, as experienced an observer as John W. Gardner of

Common Cause discerns much discontent among many varied groups in the United States. He says, "[Discontent] could lead to a splintering of the [political] parties. It could lead to massive refusals to vote. It could lead to following demagogues."

All the many aspects of our social crises are faithfully and relentlessly reflected in individuals seen in psychiatric consultation. As a sociologist, Seeley, remarked recently, the social and the individual psychological experience can no longer be divorced from one another in the treatment situation.

Many a patient begins his account of an anxiety dream with a reference to recent news developments. Of course we know that these manifest events only precipitate latent anxieties. News media are increasingly becoming prime causes of anxiety, however, especially to young people who have been living all their lives under the threat posed by nuclear weapons. School itself is in a state of crisis, as the educator Charles Silberman shows in a volume prepared for the Carnegie Foundation, *Crisis in the Classroom*. Children suffer from informational overload. Teachers pile on the data in a rote manner, themselves overwhelmed by rapid changes. Classes are too large and are often torn by social strife. Silberman characterizes the school experience as joyless and as destructive to children's creative abilities.

All these many different crises add up to the story of our day. Ours is not an average expectable environment. It bears all the earmarks of a period of major upheaval, and our psychic resources are being constantly and sorely strained as they struggle to deal with it. As in individual crises, we need to understand the critical state of our society and all the elements of the realistic and psychological responses to such a crisis situation. Once the situation is properly diagnosed, we might then be able to engage in the necessary therapeutic crisis intervention.

This leaves the question of how to analyze a society that is responding to external stress. In 1961, Gerald Caplan, a psychiatrist at Harvard, usefully differentiated more or less chronic individual problems ("intrapersonal problems" would be a better term) from situational problems and crisis reactions. The latter he defined as acute adaptive reactions to individual stress. Caplan defines crisis as follows:

> A state provoked when a person faces an obstacle to important life goals that is, for a time, insurmountable through the utilization of customary methods of problem-solving. A period of disorganization ensues, a period of upset, during which many different abortive attempts at solution are made. Eventually some kind of adaptation is achieved which may or may not be in the best interest of that person and his fellows.

When we examine the adaptive responses of an individual, we usually judge him according to Heinz Hartmann's concept of an "average expectable environment."

A number of research associates and I have been studying ego functions of schizophrenics, neurotics and normal people by experimental techniques. In our team's attempt to assess ego functions, which I will describe in greater detail later on, we have come to speak of the functioning on this average expectable level as the characteristic level. We also make ratings, however, on the level of optimal functioning, poorest functioning and current functioning. Especially in the latter rating, we examine the quality of adaptive functioning in relation to the specific environment in which we see the person. Whether under stress of mourning, or in war—as when American soldiers acted at My Lai—or in some other unusual circumstance, a person's adaptation has to be seen in the light of the special situation.

There may be ordinary times for a society—an average expectable environment. The Eisenhower years were relatively quiet ones for American society —even if they did contain, and sow, the seeds of future trouble. In distinction to that period, our contemporary society has much stress to contend with. Watergate will be an historical example.

Many societies have been studied from the standpoint of how they deal with different environmental stresses. Typically, these studies have been made by anthropologists who observed several primitive societies under the stress of contact with some variety of Western culture. Such societies could be observed to react adaptively and maladaptively. Japan is a striking example of a society which has reacted primarily adaptively to the original contact with the West and the American occupation after World War II. The Japanese originally took what Western civilization had to offer and have since managed to equal it industrially. Only now are some maladaptive dislocations becoming apparent in the Japanese society. The breakdown of old established social values in the theocratic-patriarchal system are currently producing a generational and cultural gap that is disruptive to the basic structure of Japanese society.

In our American culture, and in Western society in general, external stress has been provided by the technological advances that seem to progress now almost on their own. We are very nearly in the position of the sorcerer's apprentice who could start the witchcraft, but did not know how to stop it. How do we deal with our lives and our society before things go completely out of control?

Gerald Caplan, in *Approaches to Community Mental Health,* has spoken of four phases of a crisis. The first phase he characterizes as a summoning of the accustomed problem-solving responses. Phase two is marked by an increase in tension because the phase-one responses are not successful in dealing with the continued disturbance. In the American social scene, one might say that phase one passed into phase two when the Supreme Court held that segregation in the schools was unconstitutional. The measure was an habitual social response of the kind that worked before in resolving the emergent problems of labor and the threat of monopoly trusts. It failed to solve the racial problem in America.

In phase three, further internal and external resources are mobilized. This was done with regard to the racial problem. Martin Luther King from one side and President John Kennedy from the other tried such further coping attempts. Emergency coping techniques were designed, such as busing and the Peace Corps, as an outlet (for black youth as well as white). Under Kennedy, members of the artistic and intellectual communities were invited into the decision-making process. Kennedy's death and the tragedy of Vietnam only accentuated the fact that these devices were not enough. The third phase of crisis and an attempt to find ways to meet it are by no means over.

The revolt of students was another stress, which school administrations originally met quite inadequately, first by denouncing it, and then by capitulating. Only now has the response become somewhat adaptive by, on the one hand, introducing some constructive measures, and on the other, by controlling the lunatic fringe. The extreme of polarization of the Nixon years brought the American system close to destruction, and may have been the starting point for a resynthesis.

For the time being, however, we as an overall society are well into the fourth phase of crisis: the problem is neither solved nor is the demand for satisfaction given up. Demands *are* sometimes given up, both by individuals and by societies. There was a complete cessation of scientific achievement during the Middle Ages and a century-long lapse in fundamental changes in political structure following the French Revolution, in the period between 1815 and 1914. In his efforts to achieve détente on the international scene, Secretary of State Henry Kissinger is, in effect, following in the steps of his mentor Metternich, who tried to re-establish the political stasis disrupted by the Napoleonic Wars. The fourth phase is a very dangerous one. It is marked by a mounting tension that may cause major disorganization and eventual breakdown of the individual or of the society.

This tension is evidenced on the local scene by the unease manifested by nearly everyone. The credibility gap borders on paranoia. The city dweller's fear of crime is near the breaking point. Many news analysts have suggested that the determination to control violence and crime may be the major factor in deciding votes in future elections. Traffic snarls restrict movement in many cities and may eventually bring them to a standstill. In many urban centers, life is becoming close to unbearable for everyone. As a placid, usually optimistic, internist friend put it to me recently, "You become aware of having to push just a little harder every day just to make do at all." He had just spent hours trying to find an available hospital bed for a childhood friend who had suffered a myocardial infarction.

It is from the standpoint of crisis theory, then, that we have to view our world. We must understand the stresses, the attempts at adaptation and the dangerous maladaptive devices as well. We must first try to treat society from the point of view of crisis intervention, and then plan for prolonged treatment and prevention of the symptoms.

Psychoanalysts invented the concept of the "ego" to designate that portion of man's personality that keeps the peace among the demands of reality, drive and conscience. In other words, the ego is man's adaptive mechanism. Techniques of studying the ego have emerged slowly over the years.

For the last five years several colleagues and I have been engaged, with the help of grants from the

National Institute of Mental Health, in an intensive study of what psychoanalysts call "ego functions" in schizophrenics. I would like to consider our contemporary society in the light of what we have learned about the adaptive problems of schizophrenics, neurotics and normals, and look for some specific notions that might usefully apply to today's problems of adaptation, and that might possibly be adapted to the treatment and prevention of society's ills.

Because the ego has so many facets, we found it practical to define its various performances and tasks as ego functions. In a careful process of searching for the best organization, we arrived at the following twelve ego functions (each of which will be discussed more fully in subsequent separate chapters).*

(1) Reality testing—the accuracy of one's perception, orientation and interpretation of internal and external events;

*Of course, any such arbitrary selection is bound to have its advantages and disadvantages. Experimentation indicated that these were the twelve functions *necessary and sufficient* to encompass the functioning of about 150 people, including neurotics and normals. After collecting a good deal of background data about our subjects, my colleagues and I devised a two-hour interview that would reveal a person's adaptation to the world, and then modified it until we were satisfied that it would do the job well. We worked out a manual for the interviewer in order to insure uniformity, tape recorded the subjects' interviews, and then asked four independent psychologists or psychiatrists to rate each subject (on a scale of one to seven) for the twelve ego functions from that interview.

Numbers usually throw people off. If one keeps in mind that in essence all one has to say is that this person we are testing is excellent, the next one is very good, fair, poor, etc., it is easy to see that one could translate this statement into numbers—a very poor might get a one, poor a two, good a four, excellent a seven. We asked our raters to place each subject or patient somewhere on this scale for each of the twelve ego functions.

(2) Judgment—anticipation of the likely consequences of intended behavior, and the degree to which knowledge of the consequences influences intended behavior;

(3) Sense of reality of the world and of the self—recognition of external events as real, and their context as familiar. The degree of development of individuality, self-esteem and uniqueness. When this sense is disturbed, there is a feeling of unreality about one's identity, one's own body and the world.

(4) Regulation and control of drives—the ability to delay or control impulse, and the degree of ability to tolerate frustration;

(5) Object relations—regulating relationships to others;

(6) Thought processes—attention, concentration, anticipation, concept formation, language, logical and abstract thinking;

(7) Adaptive regression in the service of the ego (ARISE)—(creativity)—ability for deliberate relaxation of perceptual acuity and ability to reinterpret perceptions;

(8) Defensive functioning—degree to which defense mechanisms affect behavior, and the degree to which they are successful;

(9) Stimulus barrier—awareness of and response to external stimuli and pain;

(10) Autonomous functioning—freedom from impairment of basic physical faculties (sight, coordination, etc.) and ability to combine these faculties into complex patterns (routines, skills, etc.);

(11) Synthetic, integrative functioning—ability to reconcile contradictory attitudes, behaviors,

etc., and to consistently relate things to each other;

(12) Mastery-competence—actual competence in performance and the subjective sense of competence.

As in so many other neat schemes, the ego function scheme appears a lot neater than it really is. If all the twelve modes of functioning are bracketed as belonging to the ego, they obviously must have some shared common denominators.

For example, in describing a basketball player named Jones, one might say that he is so many inches tall and describe his agility, accuracy and general adaptive ability on the basketball court. Such a description, if rated on each of a number of carefully defined variables, would differentiate him from a basketball player named Smith. However, while Jones may be particularly accurate and Smith particularly fast, they are probably both very tall and both of them are probably both accurate and fast. Thus, though there are discernible differences between them, the likelihood is that their speed and accuracy are closely related. You could say, then, that they both have a high level of physical functioning.

Ego functions, too, can be scored independently since these functions may substantially differ in quality within a single person. But again, they may show enough correlation to permit a researcher to categorize a given group of people as having, generally, a high level of ego functioning.

Just as it is true in human beings, one finds in describing society that some units of behavior represent somewhat overlapping ego functions, for better or for worse. For instance, reality testing is usually quite closely related to thought processes, but not necessarily as closely related to drive control. Other functions may be quite discrepant from overall adaptiveness. It remains for us to see what pattern emerges for our society.

I propose to apply these twelve ego functions to this study of our society. They have been found useful in the understanding, diagnosis, treatment and prognosis of individual schizophrenic, neurotic and normal people.

As we approach the study of our society's response to the crisis of overload, it is important to understand that not all responses are maladaptive. On the contrary, most individuals, as well as society as a whole, make some adaptive response in terms of actual problem solving. The question is, how much of an adaptation is made and at the cost of what other functions? For instance, an individual might make very good adaptations to the rigors of battle in terms of survival, at the cost of some sense of self, with a reduction of autonomous functioning and with a loss of creativity. Our society has made a number of adaptive responses to the problems besetting us. Social security, attempts at pollution control, integration and birth control are successful adaptive measures. They are attained at the cost of some loss of individual choice. Socialized medicine is often depersonalized medicine; people against integration feel a loss of personal freedom of choice in the people they want to associate with; industrialists do not relish the expense of increased controls on waste disposal.

We will be dealing mostly with the failures of our society to meet its adaptational problems. This should not blind us to the possibility that solutions to adaptational crises can be eventually found and may result in better and more stable situations than existed before the crises. This certainly holds true for individuals. There are some *bona fide* cases of schizophrenics who emerged after a real psychotic episode much better integrated and able to cope than before.

Similarly, it is entirely possible that our society could emerge with many gains after some traumatic events. We could conceivably evolve a better distribution of justice, more time for constructive and enjoyable work, no wars and almost unimaginable social and technical progress—if we survive the crisis. Survival may take some very intense social doctoring. Thus I have come to regard the social sciences, including psychiatry, as the *survival sciences.*

I am aware that some sociologists and social psychologists doubt that certain methods that are useful in dealing with individuals can be effectively applied to groups or societies. Yet, as a practicing psychoanalyst, psychiatrist and psychologist of many years, I have found compelling evidence to the contrary.

For 30 years I have been listening to people from various walks of life. I have become acquainted with many people from the lower socioeconomic groups through my work in outpatient clinics (particularly at the Troubleshooting Clinic in New York City, which I originated and which I directed from

1958 to 1964). In private practice, I have come to know members of the upper middle class. Annual trips to Europe (and occasionally to other parts of the world) have given me background material from many different cultures. From this collective experience I have come to believe that the methods I found useful in the strictly psychiatric study of individuals can reliably be applied to the study of the adaptational problems of our society.

One can study ego functions at different periods in the development of a society or individual. Certainly regulation and control of drives, both in cities and on college campuses, was better in the summer of 1971 than in 1970, and better in 1970 than in 1969. In numerical terms, one might say that if seven represents a state of blissful perfection with regard to civic discipline, the summer of 1971 might merit a five, and the previous ones, four and three respectively.

Initial reactions by authorities to unrest were characterized by panic and disorganization. With time, however, there came an increased willingness to alter antiquated systems and to deal more firmly with destructive behavior and irrational demands, a change indicative of improved reality testing and other adaptive ego functions.

Similar assessments should be made concerning the state of other adaptive functions of a nation. Indeed, the gathering of national and regional statistics on the adaptive functions of the population should be as routine as economic indexes have become. Just as we have many different and complex forms of economic indicators, the mental state of the nation—of any nation—is bound to be many-faceted and complex.

This volume is a first attempt at gathering indexes for adaptive functions, and I wish it to be a guidepost in a critical time. For the future, I would hope that a body of social scientists—historians, economists, psychologists, anthropologists, psychiatrists and sociologists—would rate not only present but past societies as well.

chapter 3

REALITY TESTING
and the SICK SOCIETY
—Staying with It Makes One Dizzy

If a man sees Martians flying in through his window, or hears voices calling him, when no one else can see the Martians or hear the voices, we judge his reality testing to be poor. He sees and hears things that are not really there. He also may not see things that *are* there; for instance, he does not see the ambulance and the men in white. To the extent to which the men in white become the Martians in his mind, he distorts reality—fearfully, in this case.

Asleep, any of us could have such a dream. Dreams have been compared to psychoses. How do we usually decide that something was a dream? Mostly by the discontinuity between waking experience and dreaming experience. Reliance on a relatively stable and continuous system of experiences from yesterday to today helps us test reality in everyday life.

There are other time-honored ways to help one know what is real and what is not. "I pinched myself to make sure I wasn't dreaming." The idea is that if one were asleep and were to pinch oneself hard, the pain would certainly wake one up. If the visual perception persists, the assumption is that one is not sleeping and dreaming. The pinch feels real and provides the consensual validation for reality testing.

The fellow with the Martians suffers from a difficulty in distinguishing between his own internal ideas and his external perceptions of what is *really* out there. Failure to perceive the ambulance personnel as such showed his deficient accuracy of perception. The skeptical pincher tested another aspect of reality, that which we call "inner reality testing." It is concerned with the accuracy of appraising one's own psychological state. Am I asleep or not? Am I drunk or not? Am I rational or not? These are questions which one must ask oneself and be able to answer accurately if one's inner reality testing is all right. The self-doubting, self-observing attitudes, and in the long run, the willingness to accept the social consensus (if it is in conflict with one's own inner reality testing) are crucial. "If three people tell you you are drunk, you'd better believe it," expresses the idea of the social consensus versus one's own inner reality testing.

One may also request social validation. "Do you see what I see?" is usually just a colloquialism. The person who fell asleep on a sunny beach may wake up and say, "Did I dream this music or was there really music somewhere?" This is asked to help differentiate between inner and outer reality. We may get confused at times in such experiences as *déjà vu* and *déjà reconnú*—the feeling of having already seen something or experienced it, when one has reason to doubt that one indeed has.

What does all this have to do with problems of our unsure society? To start with, the rapid changes of our society make it almost as difficult to perceive reality as it is to view the real world from a rapidly spinning merry-go-round. In experiments, if we wish to make reality perception difficult, we show a subject pictures in as rapid succession as the projection mechanism allows. In the same way, the daily newspaper serves one crisis after another, before any one of them has been well understood. How can the average person really understand, and quickly, the problems of pollution, the devaluation of the dollar, the prime interest rate, the role of cyclamates in soft drinks, complex problems of Congressional ethics, Watergate, and U.S. economic policy, not to mention the economics of Russia and China?

Reality testing is indeed burdened by events stranger than fiction. French intelligence agents organize the smuggling of millions of dollars worth of heroin into the United States. Then, another French intelligence outfit, disguised as an agricultural aid agency, blows the whistle on its rival. In the process, it turns out that the French intelligence service had collaborated with gangsters in abducting and killing a North African politician, apparently as a favor to a reigning North African leader.

This kind of intrigue may sound like a movie, yet it is very real. Consider, too, the Knapp Commission's proceedings on police corruption in New York City. The Commission revealed that not only do some policemen accept bribes (as most people suspected), and then cooperatively close their eyes to illicit traffic in drugs, stolen goods and prostitution, but what is worse, some especially enterprising officers actually imported gangsters from New Jersey to set them up in illegal businesses so as to get their share in the transaction. Other police officers placed orders with the underworld gentry for specific types of liquor, cars and other items—and the items were stolen to their specifications! Can the young especially be blamed for having a hard time evaluating what is moral and what is not? How can one know whether he is dealing with a trustworthy law enforcement agent, since so many break the law?

Perception of reality works best—that is, most accurately—in a stable perspective. I once suggested to a group of pediatric residents that they walk around on their knees for an hour. The world around them would look so different to them by virtue of the changed height relationship that they would better understand how frightening the world often looks to children. The constant impact of newness and confusion, then, on previously well-established perspectives leads to perplexity in our swiftly moving society, and perplexity is, in fact, a marked feature of acutely mentally ill people as well. Even neurotic or anxious people are perplexed and thus are apt to become more anxious when confronted with too many new experiences. Some people, when they take sedatives or tranquilizers, react paradoxically with anxiety. "Paradoxically" because they *should* feel more relaxed. If one understands that the tranquilizer makes them undergo things in a new way, slowed down, it becomes clear that the mere newness of feeling themselves moving more slowly, perceiving things more slowly and having a different sensation in their muscles is sometimes enough to make their anxiety increase. It is the *usual* reaction to something new. It just happens that not everybody perceives the perceptual change due to sedatives as sharply. In turn, the speeding up of perception that is produced by some drugs, including "speed" and LSD, is often the sole factor responsible for having a bad trip, a frightening one. This sense of anxiety in response to speeded up perception is similar to feelings our current social scene provokes.

Again paradoxically, sometimes fast-moving events like the Laos incursion following the invasion of Cambodia in the Vietnam War leave one paralyzed, even apathetic. Overwhelming odds, or failure to effect any real change in existing policy despite our best efforts, make one feel helpless, as in many Eastern cultures where apathy and fatalism are the result of an unyielding caste system.

Reality in our contemporary society is confusing enough because of the complexity of society's structure and the quick changes it undergoes. Unfortunately, it is a characteristic part of our culture that the facts of reality are often deliberately made more confusing by outright distortion. This "acceptable" distortion is carried out by entire industries.

For example, false claims in advertisements, deceit in the packaging industry and misleading cues fed us by motivational research create distortion. Many publications are devoted to attempts to undo some of the distortions of reality by these and other means. *Consumer Guide* is a widely read magazine that is in essence dedicated to reality testing on behalf of the consumer. A publication called *Moneysworth* purports in full page ads to tell the true story behind a long list of commercial, political, professional and other distortions of reality. *The Wastemakers*, a muckraking volume by Vance Packard, attempted to show the destructive self-interest behind the concept of planned obsolescence, e.g., the deliberate intent to manufacture an article with poor-quality materials and shoddy workmanship as part of a scheme to force the consumer to soon reorder the same article. And Ralph Nader, the nation's leading consumer advocate, in his campaign for honest information from automobile manufacturers has wrought a near-revolution.

Distortion of the news in the political field by a variety of means is accepted since it is not special to any particular party. President Johnson was the father of the current credibility gap, and President Nixon carried on the tradition. (President Ford's actions in this regard remain to be seen.) *The Selling of the President* by Joe McGinniss gives a shocking backstage account of the Madison Avenue approach to the voter. Perceiving the effect on character of political trickery, Patrick Anderson offers the following comment on *Resurrection of Richard Nixon* by Jules Witcover:

> I cannot recommend this account of Richard Nixon's political comeback as an aspiration to the young, but I do urge it upon those mature readers who wish to ponder the uses of duplicity in Presidential politics.
>
> This is not to say that cunning alone revived Nixon's political fortunes after his defeated campaigns for the Presidency in 1960 and for the California Governorship in 1962. Jules Witcover properly credits Nixon's "fierce singlemindedness, his willingness to make a new beginning—personally and emotionally, geographically, politically. . . ." Still, readers of this well-written, well-researched book may be struck most by Nixon's sheer agility, his ability to twist any situation to serve his own ends. I know of no book that more fully documents the fine art of Tricky-Dickism.
>
> We are shown Nixon the Unifier, piously calling for party unity, while gracefully slipping verbal shivs into his Republican opponents. We see Nixon the Nimble taking a soft line on Cuba in 1960, and then switching to a hard line in 1963. We see Nixon the Patriot, a fire-breathing hawk when that seemed the best route to the 1968 Republican nomination, then deftly declaring a one-man "moratorium" on the Vietnam debate when silence seemed the safest policy [*New York Times Book Review*, August 9, 1970].

The logical extension of the reality distorting devices so far enumerated is found in authoritarian propaganda of the Left and of the Right. In a dictatorship there is no need for subtlety. Control of the media presents reality the way it wishes it to be seen. The more complete the control of media, the more successful the hoax. George Orwell's *1984* examines the classic example of this style. Brainwashing and menticide are well-established techniques in the reality distorting business of governments. Big Brother and doublethink are derivatives of the simpler doubletalk techniques.

Some of the distortions in the political arena lead to the paranoid-like reactions that we find in schizophrenics and others. Emotional reactions to distorted facts cross all party lines and are found among individuals who represent the extreme Right and the extreme Left. On the extreme Left is the overinclusive thinking of the New Left, the old anarchists and such viciously disordered people as those involved in the Sharon Tate murders in California. Because some of the features of the Establishment are bad, everything that to them represents Establishment is bad. In fact (to them and to the anarchists), political order as such is bad, and therefore every destructive act is permissible. Such overinclusive, defective thinking and twisting of reality is typical of many schizophrenics.

On the Right, the "hard-hats," along with various vigilante groups, nurture the black or white, good-guy vs. bad-guy mentality of the classical paranoid. The latter, disturbed by conflicts, finds a solution in one scapegoat. Jones or Smith is responsible for his troubles. Therefore, do away with Jones. Such distortion of facts simplifies the problem in a way dangerous to the paranoid and to society. Again, in that respect it makes little difference whether the politically paranoid system is a Marxist system or a Nazi system, or the simpler system espoused by the John Birch Society.

We need not go that far or become that dramatic to make the points about reality distortion that contribute to the problems of our society. A less serious example (albeit no less shocking) of reality distortion was revealed in a poll of residents of Washington, D.C. Asked about the first astronauts' landing on the moon, a substantial percentage of people simply did not believe that they had been on the moon. They thought it was make-believe. (Some blacks felt that this was just another attempt on the part of the white Establishment to distract them from their own problems.) This instance of incredulity is due both to distrust in authority figures and informational overload. Many people simply do not have the technical sophistication necessary to appraise such events, to judge what is possible and what is not.

A most devastating example of how reality testing has been affected by deception is best quoted in its entirety from "Notes and Comment" in *The New Yorker:**

In the last several months, the public's confidence in the government has been further threatened by the introduction of a form of offi-

*Reprinted by permission; © 1970, *The New Yorker Magazine, Inc.*

cial deception that may be altogether new in American political life. Two incidents, which represent high points in the new trend, tell a good part of the story. After President Nixon made his famous remark, at a press conference in Denver, that Charles Manson, who is on trial in California, was "guilty, directly or indirectly, of eight murders without reason," officials of his Administration issued a series of statements about the incident that ran as follows: (a) Minutes after the press conference was over, the President's press secretary, Ronald Ziegler, issued a "clarification" asserting that the President had meant to say Manson was "allegedly" guilty of the murders. When Ziegler was asked whether he was retracting the President's statement, he replied that he thought he had done so. (b) Shortly after Ziegler's statement was issued, Attorney General Mitchell, who had been at the President's side when the remark was made, told newsmen, in effect, that the remark had never been made at all. He said that he did not think the President had "made a charge or implied one." (c) That evening, the President issued a statement asserting that Ziegler's remarks earlier in the day had been "unequivocal," and adding, "The last thing I would do is prejudice the legal rights of any person in any circumstances." (d) Several days later, Mitchell said a few more words to the press on the subject, and this time he declared that as soon as the President had uttered the remark about Manson, he himself had been aware that the President had made a slip of the tongue, and the reason he had not said anything about it at the time was that "it is not the proper posture

of anybody to correct the President of the
United States when the President is speaking."
The second incident involves a statement made
by Communications Director Herbert Klein
about another of the President's remarks;
namely, his remark, back in April, that one objective of the American troops' mission in Cambodia was going to be the capture of COSVN,
which he described as "the headquarters of the
entire Communist military operation in South
Vietnam." In mid-June, as the American
ground operations in Cambodia were coming to
a close, Klein said, "There has been a great deal
of misunderstanding regarding COSVN, and I
think the briefings indicated we would capture
some of the headquarters areas. Some of these
were found in the so-called 'The City'—this
great underground complex which included
their schools and signals and everything. Basically, the key part, the general staff and the
radio, was never part of the plan. It would have
been a longshot chance had we been able to
capture them."

Ordinarily, when democratic governments
try to deceive the public, they limit their deceptions to matters of which the public can have
only a hazy and indirect knowledge, such as
foreign wars or the activities of vast, amorphous
bureaucracies. But when a government ex-
pands the field of deception to include deceptions about what its highest public officials have
recently stated before the public, as Klein and
Mitchell did in the incidents we have mentioned, it is invading one of the few areas in
political life of which the public can have direct,
first-hand knowledge. The citizen who has to

rely on the reports of journalists and politicians
for most of what he knows about public events
can see and hear with his own eyes and ears, in
his own living room, the President and other
officials making public statements on television.
He may doubt the truth of what the official says,
but he cannot doubt that the official has said it.
For this reason, a lie about a recent public statement—and particularly a televised public statement—is one of the most extreme, brazen kinds
of affront that an official can offer to the public's
intelligence. Such lies, far from concealing in-
consistencies of policy, actually flaunt them before the public. They are based on the insulting
assumption that the public can believe two contradictory things at the same time, or else that
each time a policy statement is made, all previous statements on the same subject, however
recent, are erased from the public's mind.

This new kind of lying, similar to the Big Lie
practiced in totalitarian countries—in which
the government tries to convince the public of
a grossly false but self-consistent version of the
facts—is nonetheless different, because it destroys all consistency, even the internal consistency of the government's position. In short,
the government defies and obliterates its own
word, and policy statements become unintelligible as well as untruthful. When this happens,
the points of certainty that might serve as a
common basis for constructive discussion are
lost, and the kind of rational public debate that
is essential to the functioning of a democracy
becomes impossible.

Societies, too, can distort reality. A large portion of our society perceived our interference in Vietnamese internal politics as guarding liberty from attack; some argue that if everyone were simply willing to work, domestic poverty would no longer be a problem. The "Watergate affair"—the now-you-see-it, now-you-don't account of spying on the Democratic headquarters—and the year-long cover-up that followed it, exemplify a deliberately perpetuated distortion of reality that has to confuse the firmest believer and surprise the staunchest skeptic. The sequence of strong denials that certain events had occurred, which in short order were then proved to have taken place, confirmed one's worst fears—that make-believe is a widely practiced policy in high government circles, as well as elsewhere.

Curiously, and luckily, the entire Watergate affair, the Congressional committees' televised public proceedings, and the subsequent trials seem to have had an educational effect on the American public. With the floodlights of publicity, reality testing reached higher levels than it had in a long time. The White House tapes themselves were rock bottom reality data that had a virtually stunning effect.

Until the release of the tapes, the only data available on Watergate were ill-defined and equivocal, similar in some ways to data provided in clinical and experimental psychological situations such as the Rorschach test. Sometimes we show our subjects ambiguous pictures—ink blots or human figures—and ask them what they can make of them. Because these perceptual stimuli are ambiguous, people tend to perceive them in terms of their own anxieties, hopes and experiences. We say that equivocal data tend to facilitate emotional distortion of reality. It is one characteristic of our unsure society that all information is increasingly bewildering because it is presented so rapidly and relentlessly, because it is manipulated in the style of the "Orwellian" society of *1984,* and because it is becoming more and more incomprehensible by virtue of its staggering complexity (which is, we must admit, sometimes intentional). All of this tends to blur reality, *en masse,* in contemporary society and encourage emotional distortion; its effects are dangerous and destructive in proportion to any individual's own personality makeup. But confusion tends to be "catching;" one person's rising tension level acts on those around him.

Polarization, so widely observed and justly feared, is a defensive emotional response to poorly perceived reality. By and large, people with an authoritarian upbringing tend to insist, in an ambiguous situation, that there is only one thing to be seen —namely, what they see. It is a black or white situation to them; such a person is frightened and says in response to an ink blot test that this is obviously a crocodile with a deer in its mouth. When one asks how come he sees the crocodile with the deer, he is likely to say, "Because it is there in the picture." This response may stand in contrast to statistical fact collected from thousands of other viewers of that same ink blot, the majority of whom simply saw a butterfly. The crocodile viewer tends to be the one who will accept simple explanations. In a communist society, he is the one who thinks that everything that displeases him is the fault of the capitalist; and conversely, there is the capitalist who thinks everything he disapproves of is the work of the communists.

The New Left type of person, when given a whole series of ink blot tests, is likely to say that it is all nonsense and amounts to nothing. His world is a very confused one; he has grown up without clear cut perspectives because of the prevalence of change. This problem is similar to one in which we ask subjects to look into a specially prepared room in which people and objects are so arranged that some near ones are small and some distant ones are large and other objects mixed in at random. In this "distorted room," the subject may become confused because he cannot rely on his usual visual cues.

Many of the young people who grew up in the last two decades have had precisely that experience, because of the hypocrisy they sense in the older generation with its emphasis on "do as I say and not as I do."

Authorities have often turned out to misrepresent themselves, and many of the young feel the whole Establishment is a hoax and self-serving, and, in desperation, they declare that nothing is real. They are told to respect certain traditional moral values, and yet they have experienced the war in Vietnam, the threat of nuclear weapons and the Watergate episode—all of which are deceptions that lead to a devaluation of reality and to withdrawal, depression and clinical situations. The same thing happens in the social situation. Some of the young people in the communes have been disappointed by the Establishment and are turning away from it, away from reality. The drug scene must be interpreted in that way. (I know perfectly well that it is possible for some normal people to smoke marijuana without any deleterious consequences or any pathological implications. They may enjoy the Philharmonic or other sensual experiences more under the influence of pot. Nevertheless, for the majority of habitual drug users, especially of the harder drugs, a drug trip is a trip away from reality. Even though pot and sometimes other drugs are taken in a social setting, the drug trip is still a *solitary* trip.)

Of course discontent in civilization is not new. In fact, Freud wrote a small monograph with just that title in 1930, in which he said: "Voluntary loneliness, isolation from others, is the readiest safeguard against unhappiness that may arise out of human relations. The crudest of these methods (of avoiding pain) of influencing the body and also the most effective one is that of intoxication."

In that sense, the great problem of drug taking must be seen as a response to disappointment and confusion with the realities of our society. It is the result of anxiety, of difficulties in reality perception as well as a dangerous cause of further misinterpretation of reality.

There is another large segment of the population, however, that is sometimes labeled the "silent majority." This group has reverted to the childhood notion that "father knows best." They delegate the perception of reality, judgment and decision-making to those in authority. At the cost of extensive denial of their own true perceptions, these people have given up reality testing beyond their most immediate personal daily needs.

PROPOSED REMEDIES

A young mother was greatly puzzled by an educational toy she found in a local toy store. "Isn't it too complicated for a little boy?" she asked the salesperson.

"It was made to help children adjust to today's world," replied the clerk. "No matter how carefully the child tries to put it together it won't work." Such is the world we live in. Simply diagnosing the problem is not enough and the approach of this toy store clerk is not likely to help our children learn to cope. Proper treatment is of the essence. A treatment plan for our society should address itself to the specific causes and symptoms of disturbance, as it does in the care of individual ailments.

Although the realities of our world have become incomprehensibly complex, we cannot turn back the clock or destroy the computers. We can, however, halt the overabundant production of new and unnecessary complex structures.

I submit that we need a Social Science Commission which would deal with the broad concepts of social planning. This commission can be drawn up along the lines of the FTC, FDA or the FCC in order to coordinate technology and social planning on a national level. Surely, we need "humanology" experts to examine more carefully than in the past the peripheral effects of each innovation before it is instituted. For example, the fact that the Supersonic Transport (SST) might disturb the layer of ozone above the earth so as to permit greater amounts of ultraviolet rays to penetrate to earth may be an important reason for prohibiting its use. An ad hoc committee of the National Academy of Sciences-National Research Council has testified that an increase in these rays might well result in a greater incidence of skin cancer—as well as being of "life-and-death importance to creatures from man to insect."

Beyond such technical considerations, vital as they are, this Social Science Commission would further coordinate technology with humanology by determining the social, cultural and psychological effects of any new technical development. Our emotional readiness to accept innovations, and our ability to understand and adjust to them, must be considered.

Another duty of the commission would include sampling reality testing and presenting the results to the general population in a helpful, constructive way. Fluoridation of our drinking water, for instance, illustrates how the complexity of some issues exceeds the ability of most of us to grasp the essential facts of the issue, particularly when they are distorted for political purposes. If some federal body had concerned itself with providing a clear explanation of the issue in advance of actual fluoridation, much of the political strife and extremism in connection with this matter could have been avoided.

Finally, this commission might well coordinate its activities with a similar body in the United Nations. The social sciences, including psychiatry, are the *survival sciences;* they must be used to help prevent uncontrolled complexities from overwhelming us.

The democratic process as we know it will have to be more realistically defined. We need to modernize the New England town hall meeting form, which, in its original, no longer serves the needs of an unwieldy population. As I suggest in the last chapter, television is increasingly taking its place. In lieu of the personal charisma of candidates, the candidates' programs might be stated by an apolitical commentator. With a little flight of fancy, it is conceivable that some button or lever connected to the television set might eventually register approval or disapproval the way voice votes did so originally in the Greek market place and the New England town hall.

Vital issues must also be made understandable on a simpler level. We must recognize the fact that 83 percent of our population has an IQ below 110. It takes a good deal more than that to get through college, and even college graduates cannot be expected to grasp complex issues in a field in which they didn't specialize. Political issues must be kept as free from distortions as possible, so that a majority of people can truly understand and act on them intelligently.

Since reality testing is so closely related to the process of making judgments, we will next consider judgment and how to improve the ability to make sound judgments based on good reality testing.

chapter 4

JUDGMENT

A man who thinks he can fly out a window from the thirty-fifth floor of a building, without mechanical aid, is crazy. He may well perceive certain aspects of reality—namely, that he is on the thirty-fifth floor—but his judgment is impaired. This impairment may be due to several causes—among them, drug effects or schizophrenia. He does not make correct inferences from combining the fact that he is on the thirty-fifth floor and that he has no wings or mechanical contrivance to keep him airborne. Therefore, he is in danger.

The concept of judgment implies not only accurate analysis of a given situation but also the ability to make the appropriate decisions concerning it. It is not always easy to see relationships among cause, immediate effect and ultimate consequences, even under the most favorable circumstances.

In a simple illustration of this concept, one can observe that a stone is cold, but that if the stone is placed in the sun, after a while it becomes warm. The inference can then be made that the stone becomes warm because it was put in the sun. The logician cautions that the only assumption we can safely make is a temporal sequence, and that cause and effect are conjectural. However, when such a sequence occurs frequently, or invariably, the probability of cause and effect is so high as to be sufficient for our purposes.

The fact is, however, that cause and effect are rarely so simple or restricted to a single change. The fields of methodology and logic attempt to free judgments from error as much as possible. Scientists are trained to arrive at carefully reasoned judgments, yet the history of science is full of errors. Nor are the social sciences free from disparate judgments (witness the wide differences of opinion among economists with regard to the cause and effect of inflation and deflation, and the methods suggested to control them).

Everyone is familiar with the difficulties of judging issues and making decisions in everyday life to do with marriage and career. Individual emotional turmoil, the possibility of unforeseen consequences, the chances of making a wrong decision must all be taken into account when making an important judgment (John Kennedy's decision to insist that the Russians withdraw from Cuba was such an example). Difficult at best, the process of decision-making has been made infinitely more difficult by certain characteristics of today's society. Some of these difficulties are inevitable, while others are deliberately created, pernicious and dangerous.

One unavoidable aspect, for instance, of the modern world is that people are called upon more and more to make judgments about things they do not understand. The average and even above-average citizen is bombarded with complex information derived from biology, chemistry and physics, on which he must make everyday decisions related to his choice of foods, drugs, household appliances, automobiles and so on.

Judgment of economic situations has become especially difficult. What is the layman to make of economic policy if, as is obviously the case, the experts do not agree with each other? Even at the economic summit meeting of September 1974, no agreement could be reached on what is useful or bad, or whether we are headed for catastrophe or improvement. As Secretary Kissinger and President Ford stated before the United Nations, the whole world situation is affected by one simple fact: the rise in the price of oil. The result, according to the predictions of some economists, may be another worldwide depression equal to that of 1929.

In addition, familiar positions move so rapidly as to be dizzying. Conservative Republicans, for instance, don't know what to make of the fact that "their" Nixon agreed to the admission of Red China into the United Nations. Liberals have been confused by the devaluation of John F. Kennedy and the debunking of his Camelot. A country grateful to President Ford for seemingly returning old virtues to the White House was stunned by his premature pardoning of former President Nixon.

Our judgment is further burdened by the threat that our decisions will have irreparable effects, alter circumstances beyond repair, and cause the consequences to misfire. *With less time than ever to absorb mistakes, our margin for error is becoming smaller.* Nearly every event can have global implications. With atomic power harnessed, chemical and biological warfare refined and missile and communications systems developed to a remarkable point, we literally hold life and death in our hands, whether as average citizens and voters or as decision-makers and office-holders. One bad mistake, one wrong word, could bring the end.

But there are several other aspects of our civilization that deliberately hinder full use of our powers of judgment, e.g., misrepresentation of reality (see previous chapter). We are at the mercy not of reality, but of what we are told about it.

Experimentally, it is quite easy to impair people's judgment. A classical device in experimental psychology is the small barbell. The subject is told to lift small barbells. After lifting them several times, he develops a certain mental set with regard to their size and weight. When a much larger barbell is substituted, the subject approaches it with a mental and muscle set for something heavy. The large barbell is made of thin plastic; and, of course, when the subject attempts to lift it, he falls over backward because he was prepared for it to be heavy. He has been conditioned to react a certain way but is thrown off by a purposely misleading judgment exercise.

In much the same way, the magician's tricks seemingly permit one to see what he is doing, but by careful distraction and illusory devices, he impairs the judgment of his viewers.

Deliberate attempts to misguide the public are nothing new. Many Germans claim that they never knew what Hitler was up to. While this is undoubtedly a convenient story to tell, it also holds a kernel of truth. As Hitler himself asserted in *Mein Kampf,* "by the clever and continuous use of propaganda a people can even be made to mistake heaven for hell, and vice versa, the most miserable life for Paradise." By consistently sticking to the big lie and isolating the population from other sources of information, Goebbels, the Minister for National Enlightenment and Propaganda, actually so beclouded the judgment of many that they came to believe what was told them and not what their own eyes and ears perceived. He boasted that he could play upon the national psyche "as on a piano."

The harsh facts of reality, frequently masked in doubletalk, become doubly dangerous to good judgment when coupled with society's other pressures. Pollution is, to a large extent, caused by the perversion of public judgment. Special interest groups who were long ago aware of contamination by industrial waste chose to do nothing about it, or indeed engaged in active steps to deceive the public, thereby affecting its judgment. Pollution is apparently as present in Lake Baikal in Russia as in Lake Leman in Switzerland. It plagues the Hudson River as much as the French Riviera, and Thor Heyderdahl observed the effects of pollution in the middle of the Atlantic Ocean. It is quite understandable that for centuries people discharged their refuse into the seas and oceans. Yet it becomes a major problem when whole populations in an extremely industrialized society discharge their refuse from garbage scows, passenger boats, and even directly from shore into the water.

The world-dividing issue of the war in Vietnam was basically a problem of judgment involving many factors. Will Communist influence in South Vietnam vitally affect American and Asian relations strategically, economically and morally? Will our withdrawal affect United States interests throughout the world in these three ways? What of American lives lost in a struggle where neither the strategic nor moral issues were clearcut? Vietnam seemed so far away and yet loomed so near and vital when it began to involve lives of our own young men. Cause and effect in the larger sense became difficult to appraise. Contradictory opinions and facts were added to distortions from the military-industrial complex and other military interests. When compounded with emotional factors, such as inappropriate fear of loss of face or unnecessary need to prove oneself further, we had a situation where it was virtually impossible to make a sound judgment.

A combination of desperately real problems, emotional distortion and misleading judgment explains some of the extreme fringes of the Black Panther and SDS movements, misjudgment which leads to nihilism and paranoid ideation, very much like that found in schizophrenia.

Frequently what appear to be strictly technical issues become major problems of judgment when abstruse information is not fully understood. Emotion is likely to take over, particularly if our everyday lives are affected.

The fluoridation issue is one such example. Dentists and medical scientists apparently arrived at this method as a sound and safe way of avoiding tooth decay. Somehow, part of the population interpreted this to mean that our water was to be willfully contaminated with chemical substances. Some people were sufficiently aroused to develop the paranoid idea that fluoridation was a communist plot to attack the nation's health.

Judgment is further confused in technical matters when authorities offer opposing opinions and some issues receive inappropriate press coverage for the sake of sensationalism. This is nowhere more obvious than in the areas of food and drugs.

For years the Pill had been widely hailed as a means of achieving freedom from unwanted pregnancy, greater sexual freedom and relief from serious economic and medical threats for those poverty-stricken families who frequently had the largest number of offspring. Then suddenly the new medical testimony began to creep into the news, shocking much of the population. The facts reported were that the birth control pill can cause phlebitis, embolism and some endocrine upset, and encourage the growth of cancerous tissue in susceptible people. The statistical facts apparently were correct, but the statistical interpretation of these facts caused problems of judgment. The statistical chances that any of these things might happen are actually infinitely smaller than the risk of dire side effects in certain pregnancies when less certain or no means of contraception are employed. Taking the Pill seems statistically to be considerably less dangerous to life and living than ordinary automobile traffic or alternative means of controlling pregnancy.

In the food field, the matter of additives has been so confusing that many consumers, trying to arrive at a sound judgment about them, have adopted a fatalistic attitude toward their use. One day newspaper headlines informed us that cyclamates were to be immediately withdrawn from the market. Experimental evidence was said to suggest that they could be harmful. Trying to interpret the ban, many scientists concluded that the authorities, finding cyclamates a political hot potato, were forced to deal with them in an energetic way. Reexamination of the evidence seems to have vindicated the cyclamates, at least for the present.

Out of Washington also came widely reported testimony that such a staple of our diet as our breakfast cereals are valueless. By implication they are harmful, if considered as an independently sufficient source of food intake. The cereal industry blandly replied that cereals are a valuable food because they usually are served in conjunction with foods containing vitamins and proteins such as milk and fruit. This hardly reassures our confidence in the dignity of the information process which supposedly helps the average person arrive at a sound judgment. One investigator charged that the cereal industry had befuddled the American public with its propaganda as much as Russia propagandizes its people generally.

Saying one thing and doing another has been called a "double bind" by sociologists and psychiatrists. Some have claimed that parents put children in a double bind by telling them one thing while meaning another, encouraging them to do one thing and then punishing them for doing what they unintentionally encouraged them to do. One mother punished her young daughter whom she found in a compromising situation, even though she consistently bought her clothes that were suggestive and seductive.

This parental conduct is one way to produce schizophrenic behavior. If consistent clouding of judgment can really produce serious mental disturbance in an individual, it must be viewed with alarm by the general public.

It has already become clear that it is not easy to arrive at sound judgment. Even scientists have to be trained in the technique of making judgments, such as medical diagnoses. The converse also holds true. It is also possible to bring up children in such a way that they cannot form sound judgments. Children trained to accept facts and not to question or doubt what is told them may stay in line, but later their judgment becomes impaired.

Virtually since the beginning of time, the firm belief systems that are inculcated in childhood have played an outstanding role in vitiating judgment. For centuries religious dogma, as an example of one sort of firm belief system, stood in the way of scientific awareness. It hindered acceptance of the theory of evolution, and recently, of course, it has stood in the way of population control.

In many other vital issues affecting humanity, organized religious systems indeed have served as "belief systems" which tend to influence judgment: moral judgment, judgment of sexual behavior and, for that matter, political judgment.

What is more, religious systems often carry with them the notion that only their particular beliefs are right and good and lead to heaven, while all others are bad and lead to hell or some variation of it. One has good reason to suspect that having acquired and incorporated one firm and false belief system, people are predisposed to accept other false belief systems which further becloud judgment. Thus, arbitrary judgments are made and based on right and wrong, black and white, whether the issue is religious, political, moral or social.

In psychiatry, a delusion is defined as a false belief that is persistently held in the face of evidence to the contrary. The most frequently encountered delusions are paranoid delusions—that is, the firm belief that somebody is doing one evil even if there is no evidence for it. One man in his 80's became quite disturbed because he was sure the neighbors living above his apartment were intentionally making noise at night to keep him from sleeping. The neighbors had been there for many years and had been on very good terms with him. Finally his middle-aged daughter stayed over for several nights and heard no noises at all. This did not keep the senile, terribly confused and paranoid man from continuing to maintain they were making noise because they really hoped that keeping him from sleeping would kill him, and they would then inherit his money.

The more delusions we accept in one area, the harder it becomes to judge soundly in other areas. Delusional behavior grows like rings in the water. Once the old man started believing that the upstairs neighbors were out to get him, he soon also developed delusions that the people living across the street were persecuting him. Because the policeman on the beat would do nothing about it, he felt the police were also in partnership with his enemies.

The same phenomenon holds true for society. Once the public is willing to accept one scapegoat as the cause of all evil, as the Nazi Germans perceived the Jews, it was also willing to believe that any enemy of Hitler's, however Aryan, was a traitor to the state. Similar phenomena are regularly observed in Russia and China today. Minutemen and members of the John Birch Society on one side, and the Weathermen on the other side, are motivated by similar delusions. Whole sections of the country can become set against each other. It has become vital to discourage such irrationalities on the political scene. James Reston, in his *New York Times* column of March 2, 1969, made quite clear that the role of a leader, a president, is to help interpret the news and the realities of life in such a way as to help the electorate formulate the best judgment. It is not consistent with good leadership for a leader to accommodate himself to the lowest common denominator—the judgment of half the population—in order to gain its confidence and votes.

In times of crisis, people look to the leaders of their communities and governments to define their problems and to create an atmosphere in which adequate remedies can be found. Their judgment must be the best possible.

It is not always easy to diagnose impaired judgment in a society or in an individual. Sometimes pieces of inferences are quite sound and are even based on originally correct reality testing. But at some point, cause and effect are distorted by emotional problems; then judgment takes a wrong turn.

The unfortunate mental illness of former Secretary of Defense James Forrestal illustrates a combination of personal illness and political misjudgment. In the belief that the Russians were after him, he jumped to his death from a window of the Naval Hospital in Bethesda. In this case, the judgment of an otherwise reasonable man was obviously impaired by panic of a personal nature couched in a political notion.

A person in our society who thinks that any political problem can be solved by a modern version of "sending in the Marines," by calling names or by dropping the H-bomb, may suffer to a considerable extent from not having learned properly how to draw rational inferences and to logically follow them through; instead, there is a tendency to reach premature conclusions in which the emotions interfere unduly with the inferential processes.

One of the most vital times for a nation to exercise sound judgment is at election time. The citizen must then weigh old voting habits against facts. He has to balance emotional appeal against reason. Before the election is held, during the campaign, he is exposed to powerful influences. The President of the United States has it in his power to arrange events to show himself in the best possible light. He may take a foreign trip that shows him in statesmanlike activities. His name is in the headlines daily. He can pick measures to be passed in Congress—and some to be ignored—in order to make an optimal impression on the voter.

His opponent, who is in the happy position of not being responsible for the record, can attack unpleasant facts (which he may not have been able to handle any better than the incumbent) and attempt to convince the voters that he could and would conduct the affairs of the nation in a much more satisfactory way.

These are some of the crises that call upon our society to operate with sound judgment. We will need very special measures to deal with them. Some of the steps will have to be in the area of crisis intervention, and some will have to be long-range measures designed to alter the fundamentals of education, i.e., teaching judgment to our children. These measures are necessary for survival.

Proposed Remedies

Forming judgments is a complicated mental process involving many factors, only one of which is intelligence. This process is predicated upon a sound knowledge of the facts of a particular issue, which in turn derives from good reality testing. Emotions and defenses can also exert a strong influence. Therefore, crucial to improving judgment, as we have already mentioned, is the presentation of facts in the simplest way possible. We will discuss the need for safeguards for emotional health in that context in our society later on.

There are formal, logical aspects of judgment, however, that are integral to the process of judgment per se. There are ways of learning to form sound judgments much in the same way that one learns how to drive a car or build a bridge. Scientists are not born; they are formed. They all get the training necessary to make sound judgments. The experimental method and scientific thinking, for example, are simply ways of drawing inferences from facts in a most reliable way. Everyone knows that scientists sometimes err, and everyone is delighted when they disagree. Obviously there is no absolutely foolproof way of arriving at incontestably sound judgments. All we can claim is that those who are trained in making judgments, whether legal or scientific, are more likely to accurately appraise verifiable facts.

A little book, *The Anatomy of Judgment,* by M. L. G. Abercrombie provides an admirable discussion of how medical students can be taught to make judgments. The first process is to ascertain primary facts by several techniques; that is, by observing phenomena from various perspectives under different circumstances. One such technique is by physical examination, and others are, for example, by laboratory method, by X ray and by history taking. After the basic facts are recognized, one must try to fit explanations to an observed phenomenon, much the same way one tries to put together pieces of a jigsaw puzzle. Some pieces fit together better in one way than in another; one must be perceptive and patient in trying many different combinations until the best fit is accomplished.

If, using such methods, we educate our children toward better judgmental ability, they will be better able to deal with our confusing world. Unfortunately, as the Carnegie Foundation report on *Crisis in the Classroom* by Charles Silberman makes clear, joyless learning by rote is all too prevalent in our school systems. This type of learning can do much to stifle the development of judgmental ability. Awareness of the many faceted aspects of issues can be conveyed just as clearly through the teaching of history as through the teaching of science. But in history, as in science, black and white thinking is the bane of intelligent judgment. From my experience I know that sixth graders can readily be taught to draw sound inferences and make good judgments. When this ability is taught well, the ability to make reliable judgments based on unpolluted facts will contribute to the health and stability of society, as well as of individuals.

Presentation of political news will have to be completely restyled. We cannot afford the confusion in judgment that is an integral part of the time-honored political doubletalk. I am not speaking of idealistic notions of truth, but rather about basic necessities for survival. If any form of democracy is to survive, the voter has to be in a position where he can decide on the true merits of any issue.

British politics has survived on drier stuff than American hoopla, and it must be possible to make serious politics work here when people are so troubled by the credibility gap and the political circus. Common Cause, the citizens' lobby led by John Gardner, is precisely the sort of group I have in mind to encourage serious politics. I would also hope for a news publication comparable to the *Consumer Guide,* which would provide daily news after carefully screening for truth and fiction.

During political campaigns, I would suggest that, rather than relying so heavily on "style" and other superficial personality factors, it should become general practice for both sides to engage professional speakers to read prepared position papers.

My most controversial suggestion is likely to be that candidates for high office be preevaluated and prescreened for their competence and judgment before their names are placed on the ballot. It takes training and a license to become a plumber or an electrician; until now, just about anyone may be allowed to run for any office in our government. Some basic requirements for competence, intelligence and sound judgment need to be established and met by would-be candidates, a most reasonable suggestion in light of the desperate needs of our present society.

Usually there is general concern that psychiatrists and other mental health people would arrogate to themselves the right to decide for the population who would make a good president or senator. That is not the intent. All I propose is that a carefully selected jury of psychiatrists, psychologists, and possibly other specialists, examine would-be candidates and rule out those who, in their judgment, are manifestly unstable or have obvious character defects. After the greatest liabilities have been ruled out, the democratic process would take place as usual. This professional jury may not have more than an advisory function, rather than a binding one, again to soften the dictatorial aspects. It would be a situation comparable to that in which the Bar Association makes recommendations for or against judges under consideration for higher positions.

The task of assessing a person in high office or running for high office is more complex than ruling simply whether the person is psychotic or non-psychotic. More specific variables have to be appraised. Some aspects of the personality, including those comprised under "conscience or morality" could be seriously deficient without being either technically or popularly considered psychotic, and yet still be inconsistent with functioning in the common interest. For example, a designation of a "deeply ingrained maladaptive pattern of behavior ... characterized by hypersensitivity, rigidity, unwarranted suspicion, jealousy, envy, excessive self-importance, and a tendency to blame others and ascribe evil motives to them" involves not only difficulties in interpersonal relations but also the all-important faculty for *sound judgment* and *impulse control*. If one is unduly suspicious and ascribes evil motives, one is obviously not judging certain events and some people correctly, if the majority is the measuring rod. With an accumulation of jealousy, envy and anger aroused by rigidity and unwarranted suspiciousness, outbursts of impulsivity are only a likely consequence.

Yet the question of assessment is not as complex or hopelessly difficult as it might seem. There are ways of measuring a person's ability to function that could be used in prescreening candidates. A group of colleagues and I were apparently able, subject to replication by others, to design an interview that enabled us to rate people on the twelve ego functions listed earlier, obtaining a high degree of statistical reliability and validity: that is, independent observers agreed with each other highly on how well somebody functioned. The success of this interview shows that assessment is possible.

We defined the variables carefully and formulated questions to assess them. With regard to judgment, for instance, we said that it involves the ability to discriminate, to anticipate consequences, and to behave appropriately.

It becomes apparent that the various ego functions interrelate (and yet vary independently enough from each other to warrant separate consideration). Discrimination, for instance, involves reality testing. The anticipation of consequences involves the ability to match the perceived reality with data from the memory bank. And appropriate action involves the ability to control impulses in order to bend behavior toward the goal of most desirable (long range) consequences rather than toward immediate impulse gratification.

Careful, valid assessment can be done, but I would not want to make it appear simpler than it is. In the past I have suggested a fairly complex scheme for evaluating candidates for high office before they offer themselves to the electorate. This is not the place for all the details, nor are they all worked out. Suffice it to say that a carefully constituted panel of professionals would do the evaluating, of data possibly obtained by others, and would thus be able to make objective judgments, while restricting these judgments to those too grossly disturbed or inadequate (including intellectually) to be likely to do a competent job. *Their recommendations would be similar to recommendations made by the Bar Association* concerning high judicial office. After the panel's assessment, the findings would be made available to the public, just as data from physical examinations are published. Thereupon, the candidates would be voted upon in accordance with custom and the democratic process.

If the question of psychological-psychiatric suitability of an incumbent president, vice president, or other high office-holder is raised, a similar procedure, using our ego function assessment and other techniques should be used.

The task will not be easy; people aspiring to high offices are all likely to be self-centered, willing to make some moral compromises for the sake of practicality, and endowed with a variety of other characteristics not likely to have made them "scout leader of the year" in their earlier careers. And yet, the discrimination between a *permissible* degree and a *dangerous* degree of the personality features in question can and must be made by the method which we used and some modification of it. There are other possibilities for assessment of candidates and incumbents if need be, and they may be even more elegant methodologically.

The transcripts of the White House tapes are a case in point, and an apparently spontaneous speech such as former President Nixon's farewell address to his staff and White House personnel is another good example of personal records that could be used for reliable and valid psychological inferences. We call such records primary data.

Making diagnostic inferences from "primary documents" such as letters, psychotherapeutic interviews and conversations has a long and respectable history. Unlike books, which, because of the intervention of editors and writers, may be unreliable clues to the author's personality, primary documents make it possible to perform a content analysis by a method well defined in advance, such as counting the number of certain words. If there should be a statistically significant preponderance of words referring, say, to being aggrieved, or feeling inferior or envious, the relatively reliable inference can be made that the subject feels envious, aggrieved, or inferior.

The professional stance of not judging political personalities without the benefit of a personal interview was on fairly poor ground even before the existence of primary documents. A clinician studies the person's history for clues to the present, and then makes inferences on the basis of observing and listening to the person. The history of any major political figure is amply known these days. Whatever we may not know about Mr. Nixon's early childhood history, we certainly have known a great deal since he entered politics and we sample a great many behavioral data from television. The combination of these data provides more operational, behavioral data for inferences than are available for most patients whom professionals attempt to diagnose.

A careful professional usually includes a mental status examination as well as general physical, and specifically neurological, examinations in a diagnostic appraisal. I doubt very much that a mental status examination would reveal anything that is not already known from such television performances as press conferences.

We are left with one legitimate scruple: political bias on the part of the clinicians. Skilled, outstanding clinicians drawn equally from Republican and Democratic persuasions could make independent, carefully structured observations, even with scientific controls (such as samples of other peoples' primary data thrown in for separate appraisal to test inter-raters' reliability), and I believe they would turn up with judgments of high agreement on essential aspects of a candidate's or politician's personality.

Questions of personality have played a role in recent elections—in the cases of Adlai Stevenson, Eugene McCarthy and George McGovern, no less than Goldwater or Nixon, and will undoubtedly do so again in the next presidential election. It is not too soon to refine our tools and agree to let professionals use them for everyone's benefit.

If the suitability of Richard Nixon from the standpoint of behavioral science was recently the most urgent case before the public forum, it may have been as fortuitous an historical precedent as President Eisenhower's heart attack had been years before.

chapter 5

The SENSE of REALITY
of the SELF
and the WORLD

Some people lying under a star-studded summer sky feel with awe how small a part of the cosmos they are. Others gazing out upon the majesty of the sea feel like grains of sand on the beach. Still others are struck by a feeling of insignificance and near panic while walking through the concrete and glass canyons of our giant cities. The people rushing by, the impersonality of the fixed faces, cause strangers to the scene to feel as if they were in a nightmare.

The sometimes nightmarish quality of modern man caught up in the world he made is the main theme of our society. A disturbance in one's own sense of reality has been called the identity crisis. As one feels oneself unreal, the world around one also seems unreal.

Existentialism has tried to deal with problems of identity and estrangement. Karl Jaspers, Edmund Husserl and Jean-Paul Sartre approached the question philosophically. Camus and others made it the core of their literary concern. Even in mystery fiction, the antihero (e.g., the spy who came in from the cold) is caught in an impersonal nonsensical net.

Psychiatrists have long known about these feelings of depersonalization and derealization, as they call it. If one's experiencing of the world is very unreal, it is called derealization; if one feels *oneself* unreal in relation to the world around, it is called depersonalization. Actually, the two feelings often interact and coexist. It can occur in a variety of disorders, but it certainly plays a frequent role in schizophrenia. One patient was so troubled by feelings of unreality that he often smashed windowpanes with his bare fist. The pain he felt and the blood he saw made him know he and his surroundings were real.

The sense of reality of the world and of the self depends upon whether we experience external events as real and as being embedded in a familiar context. The sense of the reality of the self depends upon our body's familiarly unobtrusive functioning and upon our own familiarity with the physical self. This sense of self also depends upon the degree to which we develop a feeling of individuality, uniqueness and self-esteem; without it a person is in a psychiatric crisis.

The identity crisis in our sick society is a result of conditions which do not permit these components of the sense of reality—familiar surroundings, familiar roles and events and self-esteem—to be as strong as they used to be. The outstanding fact we have observed in our contemporary society is that a great many changes and an ever-increasing speed of change make it impossible to experience much of everyday life as going on in a familiar context. Therefore, people—our youth especially—have felt increasingly alien to the world in which they live.

One patient complained that he saw the world around him as if through slightly opaque glass, and that this glass enclosure seemed to surround him wherever he moved. Words he spoke echoed in his head, and he was often troubled by hearing them many times in his mind before saying them, which made him feel that what he was saying was very unreal. At the same time, there was a peculiar feeling in his lips and around his mouth; he felt that they were stiff, and that he could not quite move them as he wished, as if they were not part of him. He contemplated leaving his hometown, but the thought of leaving the familiar surroundings made him very anxious. Suddenly, he had to look at it all from a new perspective. He was an unusually dependent man who needed as stable a setting as possible. His mother had actually breast fed him until he was five years old, and he depended upon a constant world around him as much as he had depended upon her bosom. His physical symptoms were brought on by the fact that he had to contemplate leaving his hometown, and the thought of leaving produced great anxiety.

A society, just like an individual, can also be beset by panic if confronted by major new developments which it cannot assimilate. As taught by our science fiction, imagine that people from another plane could really land on the earth, as Erich von Daniken believes happened in the past, and be able to nullify by their superior technological power our radio, television and our defenses. Imagine that they could read our minds and anticipate our actions. This would induce not only fright but general feelings of alienation, depersonalization and derealization. While not as drastic, role changes in today's society are nevertheless marked enough to produce serious alterations in our feelings of identity. One famous movie star I treated went into a severe panic with feelings of depersonalization when he happened to come to a town where not only had no one seemed to have heard of him, but he was also unable to persuade some storekeeper of his personal status. His experience of himself as an individual, and as a unique individual, was drastically affected.

The swift changes in our world have also caused a decrease in the degree to which one can experience individuality and uniqueness—in the sense of self and self-esteem. If a child is constantly moved from one home to another, or from one school to another, when his father has been transferred from one city to another by his company (as is much more likely in contemporary times than a generation ago), he is hardly likely to develop a sound sense of self. Once upon a time, childhood experiences were acquired within the context of a family which included usually not only father and mother but, typically, aunts, uncles and grandparents. Among the middle class, a family doctor, the grocer, the butcher and many other people constituted a rather permanent, personal, familiar environment. In today's world, the parents are often away from home; sometimes either because the father has to work far from home, or at other times because, being well-to-do, they take advantage of jet travel. Mothers, in all strata of society, frequently also work. Members of the family commonly live far apart, so that uncles, aunts and grandparents are not around. It is a rare family that has a family doctor. The impersonal supermarket has replaced the grocer and the butcher. Impermanence rather than permanence is the general key to life in our society.

School life is similarly structured. Children move in and out of neighborhoods and schools, and teachers rarely stay in one school for any length of time. A feeling of haste pervades the whole educational program. Children in high school particularly acquire a sense of being overwhelmed by their curriculum, by the tremendous number of innovations in all fields of human endeavor and by the tremendous speed of historical developments.

The speed at which changes are developing in our current society make it difficult to have the necessary feeling of being embedded in a familiar context or of belonging. Having had so many changing experiences during the developmental process robs children of the feeling of identity that becomes internalized when the external environment is sufficiently stable.

To have a sense of self and self-esteem is particularly difficult in an affluent society. A man who once took pride in being a good craftsman is not likely to have any such gratification today. In this age of planned obsolescence, there is no real place for craftsmanship. It is rather typical of our society that very little pride is taken in work of any kind. Work is simply considered a means of making a living and the complaints about the lack of responsibility and lack of care in workmanship are nationwide. A recent visit of Parisian butchers to an American automated butcher shop brought this point out strongly: people who still know their individual customers are a dying race. The French butchers cut the meat according to the technique they learned in three years of apprenticeship and take some pride in what they are doing. In automated meat factories, all the fine nuances are skipped and the personnel simply operate machines. The meat is packaged in cellophane and stored in refrigerated food bins. It is picked out by a customer without contact with a human being and paid for at the exit of the supermarket.

Impersonalization characterizes our age. In matters of sense of reality of self in the world, the feeling of being lost, the sense of the bizarre due to irrational events has been caught in recent literature, perhaps most effectively in Heller's *Catch 22* and *Waiting for Godot* by Becket. They are not actually much different from, and intermingle with, the description of psychotic experiences as described in Kesey's *One Flew over the Cuckoo's Nest.*

To a certain extent, the hippie movement was an attempt to deal with this loneliness, this sensation of unrealness. As we will see later, however, it was not an effective way of regaining an identity. More often the young people lived *next* to each other with a feeling of "live and let live," rather than really *with* each other. Their "rapping," then and now, resembles what Jean Piaget calls collective monologue more than it seems like real interchange. Piaget describes how young children at a certain developmental stage, after not paying any attention to others at all, will stand next to each other, each of them speaking his piece without any interrelationship. Only later when they become sufficiently aware of each other's differences and become less self-centered do they actually talk to each other responsively.

People in panic states, people disturbed by unrealized feelings of aggression or by feelings of great need for approval and affection, may complain that they feel unreal, and that the world around them feels unreal. In more markedly disturbed people, particularly schizophrenics, there may be a feeling that a part of the body is dead, wooden, without sensation. Some schizophrenics can even mutilate themselves without apparent reaction or pain. Others have lost all individuality, all boundaries and feel as one with the universe. They believe they can understand animals talking and read other people's minds and have other people read their minds. These feelings are a defense, a way of claiming that it is not true that they are lonely, isolated and misunderstood; they are an attempt to deny hurt and disappointment. Instead these people pretend to be happy, at ease and in communication with everybody and part of everybody.

It may well be, as we will discuss later, that a new personality type will develop due to the changes in interpersonal relations. The cosmopolitan citizen of tomorrow may not develop deep enough relations ever to miss them. He may move through life the way one usually does at a cocktail party—a few words here, a brief halt there—all a matter of first names because one doesn't know or can't remember the last name. This may be one drastic cure for the problem of alienation in the unsure society.

PROPOSED REMEDIES

The identity crisis and accompanying loss of sense of reality of the self and of the world is a prominent news topic and a cause for great concern. Erik Erikson's name and his concept of identity crisis are now popular terms. The basic problem of developing and maintaining a healthy sense of reality is clear enough. Therefore, it should not be too difficult to derive preventive and therapeutic measures for treatment where the sense of self is faulty.

Let's begin with the problems of today's American adult. At least some intellectual awareness of what disturbs his sense of identity is possible and somewhat helpful. It is frequently necessary, however, to remind ourselves of these causes in order to be guided toward solutions to the problem.

New York City had a taxi strike of two weeks duration. The first cabbie I talked to after the strike felt somewhat estranged in the very streets he had been so familiar with two weeks before. So much construction had taken place in that short time, that he, an old pro, could no longer boast that he knew every inch of midtown Manhattan. With this perceptual disturbance came a feeling of loss of competence.

Another cab driver, a middle-aged family man, complained that he could not understand today's youth. He had just driven two girl passengers, one of whom, to his consternation, had freely discussed her sex life. The girl even mentioned that she had syphilis and expressed no regret or hesitation about passing it on to men with whom she had intercourse. The cab driver was genuinely upset, feeling that his whole system of moral values was being threatened.

If you are aware of being on a merry-go-round, you are less likely to let the perceptual distortions disturb you. Today we are on a merry-go-round of rapid changes, ranging from alterations in street appearance to changing sexual mores. We must accept confusion almost as a matter of course, but it should not affect our self-esteem as it did that of the two cabbies.

We can try to be aware, too, that these changes are part of our progress, much of which is for the good. It is also important not to sink into the helpless attitude that we have lost control. I tried to tell the second cab driver that he and I were lucky to still have some structure, some sense of self. I reminded him that those two young girls had known only flux from the time they were born. The atom bomb had been exploded before they could talk. All the ensuing confusion and changing values accompanying such developments as penicillin, the Pill, widespread affluence and the Vietnam War, had had untold effects. The dehumanization of a world governed by mechanization and corporation ethics has led to a loss of human values and to a loss of identity.

To avoid a serious loss of sense of self, it is necessary to be able to examine perspectives which have gone astray. We must attempt to synthesize new configurations from the old ones and from new realities. Bombings and other random violence are the manifestations of feelings of impotence and panic. Like anarchists, some of our young don't know where to lash out or against whom and so they strike out blindly.

Intelligent, concerned older people must continue to change and adapt to maintain their own sense of self as well as to keep in touch with, and constructively relate to, young people. Attempts at adaptive problem solving are good insurance against loss of identity. By reorganizing emergent facts and stubbornly and consistently sorting out sense and nonsense, one can keep one's sanity. It might help to remember the political prisoners who have survived years of solitary confinement and kept their sanity. Most of them adhered to some fixed task, mental or physical, to maintain their perspective in relation to their new situation. They survived a period of relentless tedium, a life actively distorted by a crazy prison world. Concentration camp victims, for example, who completely lost all perspective or could not change their perceptual set, perished.

In a world which passes through rapid changes on its own technological momentum, one must try to minimize changes in one's own life whenever possible. We need not go along with every fad or change our habitat and possessions more than absolutely

necessary. Especially with regard to children, unnecessary, unsettling changes should be avoided.
Children need to develop attachments to some of
their belongings and environments. Thus a sense of
self, based upon a firm structure, is encouraged to
grow.

chapter 6

REGULATION and
CONTROL of DRIVES

When white mice are exposed to sounds of high frequency and high intensity, they develop epileptic convulsions. Other mice forced to live in terribly overcrowded conditions become wildly aggressive, while some become apathetic and let themselves be bullied. Swaddled infants and restrained dogs develop more aggression than infants and dogs with freedom to move.

Imagine how it would be to live with six people in a one-room Harlem apartment on a hot 100-degree summer day, and you will understand how overcrowding and uncomfortable surroundings lead to unbridled aggression. Our society is characterized by the development of more noise, more assaults on the senses and more contact with other people than any other age. At the same time, we have more rules and regulations than ever before, precisely because of the great amount of interaction. As in the case of swaddling, these rules and regulations further contribute to an impatience and overcharging, a lack of control.

Territorialism is an important concept. It suggests that every animal likes to have his own turf. It will usually not fight if its area is not invaded, but it will fight desperately if another trespasses. Street gangs have the same concept, for every human being needs some feeling of having his own turf—or else anger is aroused. Our contemporary society permits less and less privacy, less and less of one's own backyard.

One basic, tension-producing aspect of our society is that modern conditions expose us to more irritation in the broadest sense—more interaction, less space. Added to this is the fact that precisely these conditions demand more regulation of all aspects of social behavior, from driving an automobile to running one's business. The regulations are like a hairshirt on the body already bruised from the blows of interaction.

This basically unbearable situation is made even worse by the fact that modern youth is less well equipped to cope with the tension emanating from the primary irritation of more interaction, or from the secondary irritation of the consequent regulation, than in the past.

In previous times, in the deprived, strictly class-structured society, people were often little more than beasts of burden, accustomed to wear the yoke of their lives. The church told them to "give unto

Caesar," and the hopelessness of changing their lot within guild organizations, closed educational systems and generally limited opportunities was bred from generation to generation.

Even when these inequities were minimized, society was firmly structured around what was right and what was wrong. The family constituted a small social unit in which religious, moral and financial values were firmly established. Preceptorship at home, in school and on the job, built value systems and codes of behavior which were basic to regulation and control of drives. Each person had an established role in a stable society; he knew where he stood with his neighbors and superiors. Frustration tolerance was high.

All of this has changed. The Victorian values were replaced by laissez-faire attitudes in the raising of children. In society's eagerness to do away with shackles, the pendulum often swung too far the other way. The sensible teachings of psychoanalysis became garbled, misunderstood and misapplied; when psychoanalysts spoke against irrational punitiveness and repression of sex, they were often thought to be preaching license. Certain forms of liberal education in the home and in school were ill-advisedly based on lack of structure of any kind. The idea that sex is natural was misinterpreted to mean that there was no reason why children should not be exposed to the sight of nude parents. The fact is that the growing child is little equipped to handle excess stimulation and is bound to find pathological pathways for it. Self-demand feeding as a vogue sometimes led to badly nourished and sadly confused children. It was an unreasonable alternative to rigidly enforced schedule feedings.

The children of the postwar years were especially injured through the lack of any firm controls. Laxity and overindulgence were furthered by the parents' own changing values. The indulgence that some parents showed their children was little other than self-indulgence: I did not have—so he at least should! At the same time, real kindness to children did not necessarily increase. Tired, with interests outside the home, and overstimulated themselves, parents in our society seem less able and willing to have time and patience for their children than they did before 1950. Above all, in the current freedom of sexual and economic conditions, parents are often envious of their children and subtly or not so subtly help them confuse their values even more.

The affluent society Galbraith wrote about made for more mobile conditions in most modes of life. That is how it helped usher in the unsure society. In the relatively stable class-structured society, people were content to "stay in their place." The pre war British working class exemplified this attitude. Phrases such as "not reaching above oneself" abounded.

Our affluent society created the same kind of "appetite secretion" that Pavlov demonstrated with his dogs. The fact that more things were attainable, or close to attainment, whetted more appetites. If one clearly knows that something is out of reach, one usually does not strive for it. If it dangles nearly within reach, one may become frantic trying to reach it.

This phenomenon has led to anguished outcries in the field of racial equality. Now that blacks have many more job opportunities, better schooling and generally more freedom, some members of the white community feel they should be grateful. They are indeed incensed that instead of showing their gratitude and a continued willingness to wait for more improvements, the blacks are more militant, more demanding than ever.

The outstanding example of people who are having difficulty in controlling drives is today's youth. They are heir to all the conditions mentioned. They have less living space not only because of overcrowding, but also because the H-bomb wedges them into a limited life expectancy. They are hemmed in by increasing regulation of individual initiative in what is purported to be a society of free enterprise and unlimited opportunity. The upbringing we gave them equipped them with little structure for frustration tolerance. The world they find promotes little respect for old values, and is often hypocritical in the extreme. Therefore, "law and order" have broken down. Violence—rational and irrational—abounds.

In the sober words of Hannah Arendt, a well known social critic, in an issue of *The New Yorker,*

> An emergency is certainly at hand when the established institutions of a country fail to function properly and its authority loses its power, and it is such an emergency in the United States today that has changed voluntary association into civil disobedience and transformed dissent into resistance. It is common knowledge that

this condition prevails at present—and indeed
has prevailed for some time—in large parts of
the world; what is new is that this country is no
longer an exception.

Widespread alienation and dissolution of traditional values have increased uncertainty in our society. A society, like an individual, becomes frightened
when it is unsure. Fear leads to irrationality and irrationality, to destructive behavior.

The crisis of regulation and control of drives in
our fast-changing society has been very poorly met.
Campus unrest produced either capitulation to the
lunatic fringe or recourse to legalized violence by
police and militia. Kent State University, Jackson
State, the campus at Berkeley, are sad examples of
maladaptive responses, just as the Columbia University administration, in 1968, at first responded with a
paralysis of authority.

In the political arena, the riots in Chicago at the
time of the 1968 Democratic Convention were an
illustration of political suppression. The encouragement the hard hats were given by police passivity
and by the approval of the Administration are alarm-
ing symptoms. The trial of the Chicago Seven, the
antics of Judge Hoffman and his congratulatory treatment by President Nixon may be compared to fever
symptoms close to a delirium.

If we compare the adaptive-maladaptive features of regulation and control in our society to the
characteristics that signify individual pathology, we
are led to unsettling conclusions. The inconsistent

behavior shown by the revolutionaries and the vacillations of the authorities resemble the behavior of individuals in the early stages of psychosis. Such people may also show erratic outbreaks of violence, deluded by paranoid notions that usually have a grain of truth in them. They show wide mood swings and, sometimes, just perplexity. Elation may change to inertia; violent agitation to stupor. Above all, irrationality prevails.

The individual's attempts to resolve such psychotic states often involve the formation of paranoid symptoms. One particular person is held responsible for all the patient's complaints. Societies may well react similarly. The Nazis found scapegoats in the Jews, and America was once ready to fight "the yellow peril." The Chinese Communists find enemies of the regime everywhere whenever their economy and development falters. In most South American states, anybody threatening the privileges of the few is hounded to death, including liberal Catholic clergy.

However, American society has many advantages most other societies lack. To it belongs a basic economic soundness, a tradition of freedom and an often-demonstrated flexibility in dealing with the disasters that could have been provoked, but weren't, by such as Father Coughlin, Joseph McCarthy, or, earlier, Huey Long. There is some evidence at present that more adaptive responses are in the making. There is still time to work out remedies for the short run and to prevent recurrences in the long run.

PROPOSED REMEDIES

As mentioned before, the development of civilization is paralleled by an increase in the need for regulation and control of drives. Our problem is to adapt to this need for regulation and control of nearly every action without creating a "powderkeg" situation.

For adults, one solution to this problem is to choose forms of self-expression that do not infringe upon others, e.g., styles of dress and haircut. Greater sexual freedom within socially acceptable confines is another avenue of expression. Boundaries of some sort are necessary, however, since total freedom might very well lead to a destructive loosening of controls.*

Obviously, one can become conditioned to a very broad spectrum of socially acceptable norms. For instance, in our grandmother's day, an ankle peeping out was considered seductive. Today, mini-dressed women reveal much more than that. There may, however, be a limit to how much of the human body can be exposed before the level of harmful distraction is reached. Driving a car, or conducting a class, may become greatly hampered without some controls.

Where a reasonable amount of time is allowed for adaptation and adjustment to change, controls may well adapt to meet the needs of society.

Control of aggressive impulses may be a serious problem because competitive striving is closely al-

---

*I am not interested here in morality, only in constructive social engineering.

lied to agression. Man's inhumanity to man is largely his revenge for the indignities suffered in childhood; if we raise children without overstressing the need to compete, we will minimize the problems of control of aggressive impulses.

There are also positive steps to be taken, aside from the negation or avoidance of aggressiveness. We can help children develop a high degree of frustration tolerance. Acceptance rather than hatred of different peoples can be instilled. Student exchange programs and the experience of living with different kinds of families for periods of time already do much to present differences in a positive light. To the extent that we avoid fostering the scapegoat idea, we will also prevent the polarization of people with different opinions into hostile groups.

The proposed Social Science Commission mentioned earlier would also be concerned with measuring drive control in various sections of the country and in the nation as a whole. We already make use of economic indicators which measure the Gross National Product, consumer index and degree of unemployment. We need to gauge the emotional state of the country, using similarly useful tools. If racial tension or economic stress create excessive emotional disturbance, the state or federal government must be ready to modify the underlying causes as quickly as it is often willing and able to alter economic features of a community's lifestyle.

It is not too difficult to develop some regular gauges of the emotional state of regions, cities, states and the country. A careful analysis of any daily newspaper for the variables of interest is likely to provide a pretty sound basis for such inferences. The *New York Times* summary page has often served me as a basis for inferences for the state of the world, the nation and the city with regard to several of the ego functions discussed. One could not expect that a single newspaper would every day provide valid information pertaining to each of the twelve variables we are considering. However, a steady perusal even over a period of one week is likely to provide all the information needed in order to make a reasonably accurate judgment on the fluctuating state of a community's vital ego functions.

If necessary, local, state or federal intervention might then attempt to "lower" the temperature by decreasing racial tension, economic unrest or other factors.

chapter 7

SOCIAL RELATIONS
in Our UNSURE WORLD

Every psychiatric hospital has at least one patient who sits in a corner, knees drawn up, saliva drooling from his mouth. He won't talk or move from his position and if you raise his arm he is likely to leave it where you put it. This type of patient is called a catatonic schizophrenic. He listens to inner voices, has hallucinations and is in contact with imaginary people. In another room of the hospital might be a patient who talks incessantly, laughs shrilly and paces about restlessly. She may be a manic or an excited catatonic, but she too has withdrawn from relations with the rest of us.

Genes or body chemistry may have predisposed these two individuals to these particular forms of "copping out." The fact that precipitated their illnesses, however, was that they found the world too difficult to bear; too many conflicts, too much anxiety, too little self-confidence and too little trust in others. Schizophrenia, however, is not the only way to abandon society. A visit to any one of hundreds of campuses or to a community such as the old Haight Ashbury in California revealed youths in similar condition. They had "psyched out" on drugs—"out" meaning "out of the scene." They were on a "trip" away from the real world, which had become too much for them to cope with.

The drug scene was so characteristic of our unsettled world because it reflected the trouble people have adjusting to its confusion. In the discotheque, the frug, monkey, swim and other dances symbolized the age of aloneness. Partners danced next to each other but not *with* each other. Eardrum-splitting noise was necessary to fill the void and numb the pain, while psychedelic lights provided further distraction from reality.

In an article written for the *Archives of General Psychiatry* called "Personality Structure in a Changing World," mentioned before, I suggested that human relations were likely to change in the direction of increasing superficiality under the impact of our modern society. I also suggested that a certain kind of impersonalized humaneness would develop hand-in-hand with this superficiality. The hippie phenomenon seems to bear out this prediction. Few people remain in one place long enough to develop acquaintances, let alone friends. It is certainly common for metropolitan apartment dwellers not to know even the names of most other people living in the same building. Many suburbs have a floating population of families of corporation executives. The "bed-room" community of Queens turns over half its population every few years.

My favorite way of seeing the problem of social relations is in terms of the "porcupine dilemma." This is, as a takeoff on the story of some porcupines who met on a cold winter day and decided to give each other warmth by moving close together. In do-ing so, they hurt each other with the quills. Moving apart, they became cold again. They moved back and forth a great deal until they found the ideal distance at which they could give each other warmth without hurting one another with their quills.

In our society it is easier to hurt and get hurt than ever before. More people interact with others in more ways than previously. One result of the tre-mendous increase in interaction is the development of protective armor. Our senses are dulled by the constant impact of world events. We hesitate to move close to others because we might so easily get hurt. The armor is, to a considerable extent, the ac-cepted, established form of adaptation.

The early growth of New York City's Greenwich Village neighborhood was along the same lines as today's uninvolved communities. I think of the life-style found here as "benign uninvolvement." One might very well give the shirt off one's back to some-one who needed it. On the other hand, a person in this kind of community is usually unwilling to take on any commitment, whether it be a steady job, a long-lasting friendship or an appointment to meet some-one at a given time. The troubles with this sort of social relationship are manifold. For one thing, if this ethos were widely followed choas would follow, since ties would be so loose that everyone would have to look out for himself. And even for the individuals who do engage in this unstructured lifestyle, this kind of adaptation presents difficulties. Feelings of emptiness and even depersonalization are likely.

Drug "trips" are another way of removing oneself from too close or too painful social interactions. But for some, drugs create the danger of permanent loss of contact with reality and people.

A feeling of unreality about oneself is related to lack of a social role, for our social relations are influenced by the identity we feel, or don't feel. A person must reconcile his real self with the roles he chooses or is required to play each day. He must also integrate each of his roles with one another in order to be able to function as a whole person. Although the term "role-playing" often carries with it negative connotations in this age of amateur psychoanalysis and forced sincerity, the concept need not be a negative one. True, a role may be "put on." For the most part, however, role-playing means filling the real roles in life: acting as a father to one's children, as a husband to one's wife, as a friend to one's friends and as a lawyer to one's clients.

Adequate role-playing requires an understanding of and adaptation to the situations in which the various roles occur. As in so many areas of today's world, these situations are changing so fast and move into such uncharted regions that we frequently cannot adapt to them or even begin to understand them. The rise of the women's movement, for example, deeply troubles many women, particularly young ones. They know that they are women, but they are uncertain as to what that implies in terms of role-playing. Must they accept the old established role of woman as domestic manager and helpmeet to her husband, or must they seek financial independence? Can they combine the two roles or, as some of the more radical feminists would insist, must they completely deny the first and grab the second? At present, any or all of these alternatives are viable. Eventually, however, one particular alternative may take precedence, and no woman wants to find herself in the position of playing an unacceptable role.

As with values, man unconsciously absorbs many of his notions of role and role-playing as he grows up. He forms an opinion of what a woman should be by the way his mother acts, and in becoming a man, he is strongly influenced by his father. Again, as with values, roles are no longer ironbound by social convention. Indeed, many roles are now so flexible that a child can no longer extrapolate them for himself by interpretation of the behavior of others. To some extent this may lead to greater freedom to do one's own thing. A woman can be a nuclear physicist and still find a husband if she wants to get married. Although she may have more trouble finding employment than a man, very few people still find her job incompatible with the role "woman."

On the other hand, a person who grows up with too fuzzy an idea of certain fundamental roles may be precluded from doing his own thing adequately. A boy growing up with no experience of the role "father" may have difficulty filling the role himself when the occasion arises. A woman who scorns the traditional role of "mother" may deny her daughter the chance to play this role later on, should she want to. A child who grows up without some experience of these fundamental roles is being denied a right to play them himself if, when he is an adult, they seem right for him.

There is also the problem of the intermingling of public and private roles as, for example, in the case of an executive who treats his wife and children like office boys, or in the case of the scion of a wealthy family who, as a private in the Army, expects his sergeant to make exceptions for him.

An unwillingness to work at creating permanent relationships, possibly out of fear of the pain personal involvement risks, has made detachment a virtue and commitment a liability.

One of the most disturbing effects of this loosening of interpersonal ties, to many people, is the reduction of marriage from a sacred to a merely convenient and perhaps obsolete institution. When industry builds obsolescence into every product, we certainly cannot expect human institutions to remain unaffected. Corporate shifting of personnel is obviously deleterious to maintaining close human relations. The development of technology, generally, is at the base of shifting human relations.

PROPOSED REMEDIES

Adaptation means suiting one's mode of living to the prevailing conditions. In the case of modern social relationships, this means, first of all, acknowledging certain facts of existence, such as the inevitability of mobility in all spheres of life—geographic, economic, social, emotional.

What we are primarily concerned with is adjusting to these facts in such a way as to minimize the disadvantages and make the most of the advantages.

As some degree of apartness seems inevitable, it is important to make the most of times and occasions of togetherness. Too many of us pass each other like ships in the night. How many wives and husbands really communicate? Life is difficult enough; why should spouses, other family members and friends maintain walls within which they live uncomfortably? Obviously, frankness at all costs and all the time is not the perfect answer. A group of early, enthusiastic psychoanalysts around the turn of the century chose to free associate with each other and even included dream analysis in this interchange. The group did not remain friendly for long!

Some reasonable balance between separateness and togetherness must be found. In our society of enforced tangential relationships, the emphasis on free and close contact should be increased. The marriage relationship is a good place to start. Many husbands have to travel on the job or work late; many wives are involved in community projects or working. When they are together, shouldn't they talk to each other, rather than read the paper or talk on the phone? If they have an opportunity to share a quiet dinner together, why should they spoil it by inviting a dozen friends to join them? Similarly, they should take advantage of opportunities to relate to their children. Some parents get annoyed just by being in the same room with them. While father and mother are trying to balance the checkbook or plan a shopping list, the children may be full of questions and comments. However, when families are in a room together, they should do things together, reserving time to attend to other chores privately. I once encouraged a man to reserve fifteen minutes a day for his daughter. This arrangement led to a vast improvement in their emotional relationship which had previously consisted of spending two hours in juxtaposition without ever giving one another full attention. We can successfully counteract apartness by more intensive togetherness.

Still, there are ways to minimize separateness. Corporations *must* refrain from moving their executives about like pieces on a chessboard. Job transfers among companies could be minimized, and the virtues of remaining at one college or in one business for a reasonable length of time should be emphasized. A feeling of permanence is essential to building lasting relationships. By the same token, objects should be built to last, rather than for obsolescence. Psychoanalysts, for example, speak of object relations as encompassing both animate and inanimate objects. A doll or a blanket are a young child's "objects" and they mean security. A house or a piece of furniture can have the same meaning for adults. The feeling of identity fostered by familiar surroundings and objects furthers one's ability to relate to things as well as to people.

The fad of sensitivity training and encounter groups has a solid base in the sense that these groups accurately perceive the superficiality of an overwhelming number of relationships and are making some attempt to counteract the dissolution of ties in our society. Unfortunately, these groups tend to cater to morbid needs for exhibitionism and voyeurism as often as to more healthy needs. If run by experts rather than by self-appointed apostles, however, sensitivity training and encounter groups dealing with school and job and some family counseling may in some cases help improve relationships. They may also serve to counteract the tangential encounters we are faced with every day.

The enjoyment of sensuousness, whether sexual or gastronomic, has, of course, its rightful place, all sensational exploitation aside. Impersonal sex—as well as raw-on-the-inside-but-burnt-on-the-outside hamburgers—should be replaced by a desire for real love and gourmet cooking. We must slow down our pace of living in order to permit these things to develop.

Children must be raised to tolerate differences and not let them stand in the way of friendships. To some extent our fast-moving, cosmopolitan society will cause chauvinism and intolerance to decrease simply because of the greater degree of interaction between many different peoples.

We must struggle to avoid dehumanization wherever possible. Certainly our computerized systems, from the checking account to social security, seem to reduce us to mere ciphers. Much of this is irreversible simply by virtue of the population increase. A certain amount of depersonalization is also inevitable in medicine. Because of technical advances and larger numbers of people, the neighborhood family doctor has largely disappeared. If it were up to some medical technocrats, anyone ill enough to need a home visit would automatically have to go to a hospital. There he would be shunted from computer to technician to specialist to home or to morgue, without a human contact worthy of the name. Modern medicine does provide tremendous advantages over the old-fashioned practice of medicine. Nevertheless, contact with one doctor who serves as coordinator of special services and who gets to know the patient as a person, is essential. Medical technocrats are fond of studies which show the inefficiency of neighborhood medicine. There have been no studies as yet of the number of patients who have been hurt or killed simply by virtue of the fact that the computerized hospital technician posing as some kind of professor of medicine did not know anything about the human environment of the patient.

In the field of mental health care if we are not careful, Russian community mental health facilities may well point the way for our own development. Their organizational setup is often superior to our mental health centers, but the quality and sophistication of psychiatric treatment is very poor. Community mental health programs have often been described as systems of health care delivery: it seems to me that we might soon arrive at the equivalent of a splendid postal system with no goods or mail to deliver.

There are those who see the family as the nucleus of an authoritarian setting and as an obstacle to free social relationships. Despite forecasts of its disappearance, however, I feel that the family will remain the cradle of social relationships. Some loosening of family ties in our society has been and will continue to be inevitable. More women will go to work and some will choose to have children without getting married. Greater tolerance of freedom for spouses within a marriage framework also appears inevitable. However, although family attachments are considerably looser and less restrictive than they were 30 years ago, it is unlikely that something better than marriage and some kind of nuclear family will develop. Unless there is a much more radical change in personality than seems in the cards at present, a certain degree of exclusive rights in personal relations is likely to remain. It seems that when the chips are down, one needs to be able to count on someone to be there who feels somewhat responsible as well as affectionate. Beyond that, marriage may, in the future, evolve into a much looser arrangement than we now know it.

Actually, "looser" may not be the best term. Marriage until now has often been more a form of "next-to-each-otherness" rather than togetherness. Many spouses rarely, if ever, have intimate conversations concerning their fears, hopes and desires. Sexually, a majority of spouses have remained extremely inhibited and distant. I know of sophisticated, intelligent people who dress and undress in a closet. The idea of striving for maximal sensuous as well as emotional intimacy has all too often foundered on inhibitions still part of the conception of sensuality as dirty and sinful.

In that sense, marriages have been very loose associations without needing to be. They may become looser in another sense, namely, in terms of actual time shared—be it because of job demands, travel or the increasing independence of women who, in the old days, used to spend most of their time waiting for the husband to come home. With economic opportunities, women's dependence may also greatly decrease, and the traditional patriarchal organization of the family may evaporate even more than it already has.

It is very likely that this type of apartness will lead to much more extramarital sexual activity than has been customary until now because opportunities will be more available and separations will be prolonged. If that development should come about, such marital separateness will have to be offset by an increased intensity of marital togetherness. The inner space will have to be more vigorously cultivated as the outer spatial relations loosen.

chapter 8

THOUGHT PROCESSES
and Their More Typical
DISTURBANCES

On a tropical island in the Pacific, Wolfgang Köhler, a famous psychologist, kept a number of apes for experiments on the processes of thinking. One of the classical experiments involved giving the apes two sticks. Several bananas were placed outside the cage. The apes were eager to get to the bananas, but each one of the sticks was a little too short to reach them. After many attempts, one ape was observed to fit two sticks together lengthwise and triumphantly scoop in all of the bananas. This experiment is held to demonstrate learning by insight. What went on in that ape's mind at that moment of realization is what psychologists have sometimes called an "aha" experience. As if a light suddenly flashed on in his head, he saw a new configuration, namely, instead of two short sticks and bananas out of reach, two sticks together long enough to reach the bananas. This type of thinking involves the ability to rearrange known parts into a new whole. The same thinking takes place in solving crossword puzzles. Chess players use this process for conceiving new plays, and every handyman and tinkerer has such experiences.

Psychologists, as scientists, have spent much time debating (and even fighting about) whether all learning is, in essence, of the "aha" type, or whether other forms of thinking play an essential role in mastering our environment. Chances are that several forms of thinking usually exist side by side. Even in the case of the ape, it can be said that he had engaged in *trial and error* before having his "aha" experience. One tries and makes mistakes and tries again until, if all goes well, one succeeds.

Of course, in our increasingly complex world, there is less and less of a margin for error, and it is fundamental that our thinking be as efficient as possible.

Thinking is not a simple process. It calls into play a number of other abilities such as attention, the ability to concentrate, anticipation and memory. Most of the time, thinking involves a language, though it need not be an ordinary language. It could be the symbolic language of mathematics. In order to learn from past errors, a memory bank is necessary. Computers share with us the ability to deposit data in a memory bank. Both in the human brain and in the computer, thinking must involve the ability to select or scan relevant material until one finally comes up with the right answer. The process does not work much differently from the process in a juke-box. Once you put your quarter in, you can see the needle hover until it stops at the record you chose. The machine had scanned electronically and come up with the right answer from its memory bank.

In some ways, thinking is a process similar to putting one brick on top of another to build a house. Bits of memory are like mortar, steel beams, pipes and the hundreds of other things that constitute the finished house. But, in order to build efficiently, one has to be able to find promptly what is needed. The problem is that our modern house of thought has become an extremely complex structure and is becoming even more complicated. One of the many crises of our day is the information explosion. The amount of information available by virtue of the progress of science and the increased input of data from all over the world has grown by geometric proportions. The difficulty shows up especially in schools. The memories of young children, graduate students and students in professional schools who are taught all of the new relevant information (much of which did not even exist five or ten years ago) are bound to become overburdened. The danger that memory storage will become excessively cluttered is getting greater all the time. Much greater demands are put on the retrieval system, as well as on the storage capacity.

One sign of the "retrieval system" crisis is belea-guered humanity's burgeoning dependence on computers and other devices. Another sign is the great number of advertisements about courses in memory training. By such techniques, salesmen, technicians, etc., may become storehouses of large quantities of very readily available retrievable data. There is nothing wrong with these techniques per se, so long as we keep in mind that such a need for improved memory also clearly demonstrates some of the dangers inherent in the information explosion and the attempts to deal with it. If rote memory is stressed, we may easily develop automatons who are only able to store information well and retrieve it at command. If memory is trained without sufficient emphasis on breadth of information and understanding, it will indeed only succeed in creating robots. Creative thinking, which we will discuss in the next chapter, demands an extra ability to take different parts from the memory bank and combine them into new, adaptive, creative wholes.

To think also means to be able to anticipate, to know what is likely to come next and to plan for it. Abstract thinking is the ability to find some common denominators among a set of facts and to anticipate, among other things, the next step. Our world of today makes anticipation, like almost everything else, more difficult than ever. For instance, how often does each one of us drive on the highway without ever finding a very necessary sign, or instead finding a very confusing one? I know many places where I can observe accidents or near-accidents because people are surprised by a branching off of the road and who then have to veer into another lane much too abruptly. Too often, the signmakers who are charged with alerting us to exits and interchanges fail to locate the road markings properly. Given today's intricate highway networks and high speeds, such planning failures deny drivers sufficient advance warning to change lanes safely and otherwise prepare them for shifting traffic patterns.

Many of today's problems, from pollution to overpopulation, are the direct result of insufficient ability to anticipate secondary and tertiary effects of much of our society's activities.

Abstract thinking also involves detour behavior. A child who wants to get at a piece of chocolate behind a kitchen bench has to learn, after he finds out that he can't get under the bench or climb over it, to walk around it to get at the desired sweet. This is a simple form of detour behavior. Much more complex forms have to be learned by everyone growing up in our culture, and intelligent detour behavior has to be exercised most of the time in order not to make some serious social errors. Of course, one particularly vicious form of detour behavior, which has been observed by anyone who has ever been connected with a large institution, be it corporate or political, is the technique of "going through channels." This involves social judgment and often social intelligence. It is, in addition, a useful example for illustrating the pitfalls inherent in developing excessive skill at detour behavior. Too much attention to the tricks of detouring might eventually completely interfere with one's ability to cut through the proverbial Gordian knot to arrive at a new and viable solution. It is for this reason that people who are relatively inexperienced in a given field may frequently come up with breakthroughs which the old hands have overlooked because they had become so mired down in the distracting minutiae of bureaucratic game playing.

The average person is capable of some anticipatory thinking. To a certain extent, excessive anticipation can lead to rigid mental sets. Expecting from experience that certain situations will evoke certain types of behavior may make one totally blind to the possibility of other kinds of behavior. If one remains open to unanticipated events, one may be able to be creative. When Konrad Roentgen found, to his surprise, that some of his photographic plates showed some interesting fogging and circumscribed shapes, he was intellectually flexible enough to infer that this might be the result of radiation effect on the photographic gelatin. Another negative aspect inherent in anticipatory mental sets is the fact that when a person may require new mental sets he may become extremely emotionally disturbed. Experimental animals trained to anticipate certain laboratory phenomena may show all signs of neurosis if confronted with new sets of facts which they are unable to deal with. One well-known set of experiments along these lines was conducted by the psychologist, Hobart Mowrer, who trained rats to turn off an electric shock by pushing a lever with their noses. They were then trained to stand on their hind legs to turn it off. And when that began not to work, they reverted to the attempt to push the lever with their noses. When none of these techniques were successful, they would often just withdraw into a corner and chew their feet.

The severest test of the intelligent exercise of anticipatory thinking—by average citizen and government alike—is in the area of political judgments. It is complex material at best, whether relating a local construction project to its effect on real property taxes or attempting to carry out international policy. Like it or not, we may find ourselves increasingly reliant on computer technology to make such plans for us so that desired programs can be implemented while simultaneously averting unanticipated undesirable side effects.

Judging from what Pulitzer-prize-winning reporter David Halberstam wrote in *Making of a Quagmire,* our troubles in Vietnam might primarily have been conceptual ones. He suggests that our military planners persisted in thinking of structures—bridges, trails, arms depots—while actually fighting an enemy whose strength lay in ideas and in the absence of structures. Indeed, it seems that the tragedy of Vietnam may have been to a large extent a result of our traditional concrete thinking as opposed to the Eastern facility for dialectic abstraction and mobility in thought. The North Vietnamese apparently opened a new trail as soon as an old one was destroyed. They moved supplies on bicycles and preserved a mobility that rendered the immense American firepower as tired and ineffectual as a shadow boxer. Your opponent moves away before you connect.

The fact is that not only our military strategists but our whole American culture tends to think in concrete terms. Abstractions, even political abstractions, let alone ideology and philosophy, find less of a home on our pragmatic shores than anywhere else.

Another, and primary, element in all thinking is the ability to pay attention. Attention is, after all, *the* input mechanism. Storage in memory and retrieval for anticipation are dependent upon the quality of the input in the first place. Everybody has his own attention span, but today it is being overwhelmed by the acceleration of events. Our difficulty in maintaining attention lies in the fact that we are being bombarded from all sides by information, noise and activity, which causes an attention overload. One has to be able to scan the inferences successfully, or else chaotic conditions will follow. This condition of modern life may not be too dissimilar from the feeling someone might have who had had too much to drink or who had been hit on the head: things would seem blurred, unconnected, puzzling and frighteningly unintelligible. The experience of psychotics is much the same, although for emotional reasons.

Proposed Remedies

Most people believe that thinking is a natural capacity one is born with. The fact is that abstract thinking, as engaged in by intelligent members of Western civilization, is a craft hard to come by and the result of long development—which gives us some hope that it may be developed to ever higher levels in the future.

The development of thinking and language are closely allied. It may not be true that all thinking takes place in verbal forms, but most of it does. In ancient civilizations the characters of writing, whether cuneiform, hieroglyphics or archaic Chinese, were in essence miniature pictures of the objects they meant to refer to. Thus, the symbol for a tree would resemble a tree, and the word for a man would look like some image of a person. As time went on, people learned to express thoughts in sentences without using verbs or all the fancy aspects of our contemporary language such as prepositions, conditional clauses and the lot. They managed to express relatively abstract meanings by concrete symbols. (Heavy emphasis should be on the word "concrete.")

In our contemporary culture, thinking in terms of imagery still plays a marked role in our dream life. Dreams, like the language of primitives, frequently express thoughts by an arrangement of images. Dreams are not able to connect subclauses. Dream interpretation, as taught by Freud, is in essence a way of translating the concrete language of primitive thought into abstract thought. Very often two or three dreams which follow each other consecutively in one night are like subclauses in a sentence, which psychoanalysts have learned to interpret as connecting statements. Symbols and dream images (and images in poems) are relatively loosely used vehicles similar to the loose meanings in primitive language that may have a variety of meanings depending upon the context in which they are used.

Children start out virtually on the level of primitive cultures. Possibly with the help of phylogenetic intelligence, and with the aid of growing up in our culture, they pass within a very few years through the phases that modern man has taken thousands of years to go through. Some children develop with more difficulties and some with less, but all children of at least average intelligence follow essentially the same pattern. To start with, they, like primitives, use only concrete terms, nouns—no verbs, no adjectives. Sentence structure is at first very simple. Then gradually they go from simple sentences to the more involved clauses. Language, in fact, is used for communication only after the age of three. Earlier than that, as the famous Swiss child psychologist Piaget describes children talking on a playground, it is collective monologue; that is, each of them speaks, but not necessarily to each other. There is no real experience of an exchange. Only after awhile does speech involve give and take.

Children who are not endowed with at least average intelligence may never come to use many abstract words and may never, even as adults, be able to express many abstractions. Any writer, particularly newspaper writers, will tell you that it is essential to write simple, declarative sentences. The *New York Daily News,* for example, deals little with abstract ideas because their readership, primarily of average intelligence (90–110 IQ), either would not understand them, or would find it too much labor to understand them or would not care to attempt to deal with them.

One consequence of difficulty in abstracting is a concomitant difficulty in reconciling opposing positions on an issue. Very frequently the argumentative presentation of opposite views reaches no higher level than an increasingly louder repetition of the stated position of both parties. They are usually not able to reconcile their differences in an abstract way, or at least to arrive at some syllogism that would make clear where the difference lies.

There are those who maintain that at least some people have become psychotic because they have never learned how to use language and abstract thought. There is the school of thought of G. Bateson and J. Ruesch, psychiatrists, who believe that some children are brought up in families where they are semantically confused by being verbally taught one meaning of behavior and the opposite meaning by actual conduct, a semantic confusion called the double bind. As a matter of fact, a large percentage of the psychiatric community considers a thought disorder the outstanding criterion of the schizophrenic condition. While I do not believe that this is necessarily so, I do agree that it plays a major role. I believe that there are schizophrenics who do not suffer primarily from a thought disorder, but from a problem to be discussed a little later on; namely, that of synthetic function. I agree, however, that the presence of a thought disorder in the absence of any organic disease usually implies the presence of a schizophrenic syndrome.

The main point could be summarized by saying that thinking is something that can be learned better or less well. While there will probably always be people of different intelligence, it appears entirely possible to train people of even relatively modest intelligence to think more clearly than they are accustomed to. We touched on this subject when discussing judgment, and judgment, of course, involves thinking. Educators have the primary responsibility of helping train people better able to deal with the thinking problems presented by our modern society —whether they be problems of memory, attention, anticipation or the hierarchical thinking—the logical progression of facts and ideas—that are necessary for the optimal abstractions. Teaching the "new math," for example, is one attempt to teach a logical process —in this case, in terms of mathematical abstractions. Harvard psychologist Jerome Bruner especially has insisted, and has apparently convinced a great part of the educational community, that children can be taught to think effectively and to attain to the abstract manipulation of mathematical symbols at a much earlier age than customary. Modern visual aids and learning machines are also methods that attempt to increase the amount of data stored in the memory banks, as well as to teach better retrieval methods. The entire educational process—whether in history, science, mathematics or any other field—will have to devote itself increasingly not only to the content of the subject matter, but to the process of abstract thinking that is ultimately responsible for arriving at the final conclusions.

chapter 9

CREATIVITY

Creativity is the art of adaptation. It means to make something new out of previously existing parts. This holds true for creating children as well as ideas. The creative person combines parts with which everybody is familiar into something new that leaves the onlooker astonished.

Usually, people think of creativity as a word that has to do, not with their own lives, but with the longhaired composer, the mad scientist, the wild-eyed poet. The fact is, however, that the creative act is a part of everyday life. The handyman who fixes the vacuum cleaner with a piece of the sewing machine, the cook who concocts a good meal out of last week's leftovers—they also show creativity. The Sea Bees were famous during World War II for their ability to improvise creatively.

To be creative is to engage in at least two processes: first, the outlines of the problem should be allowed to become fuzzy enough for them to be seen in a new relationship (that is, stepping far enough away from a scene may bring out entirely different features than are apparent from close up). If the scene itself is no longer entirely sharply defined, images from our own mind and experience impose themselves on it in the same way we tend to see clouds in highly personal configurations. If, in a second step, we can combine the newly perceived but still fuzzy outlines into something that is once again sharply defined, but that is scientifically, artistically or pragmatically new, we have been adaptively creative. When this happens, we, as well as those who have been attending to this process, or those who are familiar with the particular creative process and product, have an "aha" experience.

There are some people unable to permit themselves the dimming of contours, who are always reality-bound; they think concretely and therefore do not have inspirations. There are others who have many inspirations but who never get to the second phase of seeing their ideas sharply enough to make them concrete and adaptable to the various needs of reality. In a broad overgeneralization, one could say that there has always been a tendency on the part of the European intellectual to be too good at the first phase, to have many new ideas (even if many of them are woolly, impractical and imprecisely stated). European science is full of professional characters with ideational quirks. An occasional quirk actually leads to adaptive innovations. On the other hand, Americans tend to have relatively few entirely new insights in most fields, but are excellent in taking some fuzzy

European insights and adapting them to the needs of reality. It has often happened during the last few decades that the original ideas in medicine, and especially in psychiatry, have come from a European, but that the application of the idea to practical problems has found its widest field in the United States. With some qualifications one can say that the sulfa drugs were originated by G. K. Domagk in Germany, and penicillin was created in British laboratories, but both were most widely applied, studied, and mass produced in the United States. Some psychotropic drugs came from France, some, including LSD, from Switzerland. Psychoanalysis came from Vienna, but certainly reached its highest point in the United States. Electroshock treatment came from Italy but found its widest use in the United States. The latest in the psychiatric armamentarium, the lithium treatment of mania, was originated by an Australian.

Laqueur, in his comparison of pre-Hitler Germany and the contemporary American scene, suggests that the Weimar Republic, while drawing only on a few thousand people, actually was of infinitely greater creativity than contemporary American culture. In the field of literature he compares *Portnoy's Complaint* by Philip Roth to Thomas Mann's *The Magic Mountain,* and points to the renaissance of Weimar art, including Brecht, Grosz, the Bauhaus, etc.

Our age has been known for its tremendous creativity. The atomic revolution, the advances in travel, communication, medicine and the arts (however uneven the latter may be) have been heady and impressive. It would only be oversimplifying slightly to say that most of the adaptational problems in science are due to the discrepancy between the rapid and ebullient creativity in the field of the physical sciences and the lack of progress in the social sciences.

Thus creativity in physics has led to atomic power capable of world destruction, while we have not yet attained the socialization and control of drives that would permit optimal adaptive uses of this power and prevent the danger of massive destruction. Similarly, international treaties have not kept up with our explorations of the oceans, the air, and even interplanetary space.

Contemporary art is another sphere of tremendous innovation in recent years, but also suffers from a lack of phase two—i.e., self-actuated—creativity. In its attempt to reflect the confusing and devastating effects of the many crises of contemporary life, it has perhaps left too much unresolved. The very idea of "conceptual art," which is now in vogue, implies that the idea itself suffices, and the adaptation of the idea to reality through actual construction is superfluous.

Amid the Campbell soup cans and sculptures resembling doughnuts and even Swiss cheese, it is often hard to say where art genuinely reflects the loss of identity in our culture and where it simply represents humbug. Pertinent enough is the story of the mislaid doorknob that found itself in an admired spot at an exhibition at a museum of modern art.

And yet there are many artists working in all spheres who delineate space, light and ideas in new ways. Miró and Picasso attempted to get away from the traditional representational. The fauvists had a new look at our world. In photography, people like Feininger tried to catch the spirit of the times in pictures of factories and machines, while others like Carl Mydans depicted the struggle of the twentieth century on the battlefields and in the streets.

At its best, modern art indeed attempts to reflect the many conflictual processes in our daily lives. It is only reasonable that some of the experimental attempts to deal with new media, new facets of our experience, new ways of looking at experience itself should be less than satisfactory. In the long run, it promises to lead to valuable new means of experiencing and communicating these experiences.

In literature, the ferment of change has led to similar attempts at dealing with them adaptively. Ibsen and Shaw tried to portray these societal changes, as did Dreiser in America and Gerhard Hauptmann in Germany. Dreiser's successor in the "realistic" school, in distinction to the prettiness and artificiality of early literature, is probably best found in James T. Farrell in his outstanding work, the Studs Lonigan series. Curiously enough, this realistic description of hardship among the Irish-Americans 25 years ago finds its continuation currently in such "Jewish" literature as Roth's *Portnoy* and the *Herzog* of Saul Bellow. *Catch 22* in turn is a brilliant, albeit headache-producing, attempt to show the absurdity of modern life as reflected specifically in the Army.

The many stories and books without structure, content, or narration, on the other hand, represent little more than the ink blot used by psychologists for eliciting individual interpretations. Ink blots may be useful, but they are not art, and there is room for some serious doubt that *Waiting for Godot* is much more than an ink blot. The "theater of the absurd" and "black comedy" accurately echo some of the turmoil of our times. If well done, they force one to contemplate our lives in an attempt to come to some personal solution. But much of the current theater proposes simply to involve without comment. The only value judgment exercised is the selection of the specific topic offered for our viewing. It is likely that such art productions show the lack of synthesis in our educational crisis and the inability of the artist to exercise enough of a synthetic function to deal in a more structural form with the problem he chooses to ponder.

One element of the disturbance of values in our crisis culture might be the disproportionate role homosexuals have played in the arts. Their hypersensitivity not only to problems of homosexuality per se, but also to the cruelty and misery of much that is common human experience can be seen especially in the theater. Some of Tennessee Williams' best plays, for example, are the result of his own exquisite sensitivity. Theater investigating the specific problems of homosexuals themselves, such as *The Boys in the Band,* has a very legitimate place not only on the contemporary scene, but in the continuum of human experience.

Perhaps the most striking instance of homosexual influence in the arts, however, has been in contemporary fashion and design, both in men's and women's clothes. In women's fashions the leading designers have tended to underplay the female body by creating hipless, breastless dresses on the one hand, and bizarre see-through dresses on the other, neither of which are terribly flattering. The mini-skirt was permitted to slip in, but the fraternity attempted to get its revenge with the midi, which is likely to make a majority of women look bowlegged, if not dachshund-like. The current popularity of pants, on the other hand, simply represents the increasing freedom of women in our society and their advancing role as workers for whom slacks are both comfortable and practical.

The rather sexless look of much of women's fashion has its counterpart in men's clothing, which de-emphasizes masculinity. Men's fashion now favors narrow shoulders and broad hips rather than the excessively cotton-stuffed shoulders of earlier years. And today's men's slacks are often designed to be too tight both for comfort and for getting one's foot into.

To a considerable extent, these peculiar developments in fashion speak of the struggle for role identity of males and females in our quickly changing society. Body shirts and fancy Edwardian gear for men, and widespread proliferation of dungarees for both sexes indicate a tendency toward "unisex" that reflects the confusion of values and roles in our lives. Women's Liberation is yet another manifestation of this sexual upheaval.

The swift changes in our society have blurred formerly rigid rules and standards and brought about an increased tolerance for ambiguity that goes hand-in-hand with an increased creativity in many areas of daily activity far beyond simple freedom of dress or personal style. Innovative cooking has flourished with the spread of international cuisine through travel and the media. And recent economic adversity has become a spur to creativity on the domestic scene. Do-it-yourself courses and how-to books are popular, and instruction is available on such diverse subjects as repairing cars and the nearly lost art of restoring old furniture. Certainly it will take all the creativity everyone can muster to help us adapt to the problems of our world.

PROPOSED REMEDIES

The fact is that creativity is one of the ego functions that is, generally speaking, *not* in trouble in our society. On the contrary, especially in the sciences, creativity is unusually high, and to a certain extent the same can be said of experimentation in art and literature. The only problem presented by this creativity is the relative lack of standards and values it is currently spawning, as represented by a few extreme cases of seemingly intentional, outrageous maladaptation. This problem, however, is likely to correct itself of its own accord—since the vast majority of the country can in no way relate to such offensiveness and/or absurdity.

Encouragement of the public to arrive at its own standards without being taken in or misled by capricious artists and fad-following critics in these fields seems the only necessary step.

chapter 10

DEFENSE MECHANISMS

Psychological defenses are the mechanisms used to ward off unpleasant realizations about ourselves, about others or about any aspect of reality.

There are many forms of defensiveness. For instance, I started to write this chapter on one of those rainy days when it seemed best to sit down for an hour with a good detective story, and maybe have a drink, before getting down to discussing some of the more troublesome human foibles. I was probably kidding myself. A fancier name for that thinking is "rationalization," or perhaps "denial." I was denying that I really wanted to take it easy and be somewhat lazy; I was rationalizing that the hour of light reading with a drink in hand would put me in better shape for working. While this might hold true at times, I became aware that I was using these thoughts as defenses this time and succeeded in going on with the chapter. Most of the time, however, one is not aware, one is not even conscious, of the various defenses brought into play. That is what makes these defenses particularly dangerous.

Another sort of defense is illustrated by psychologist R. R. Sears's well-known experiment, in which the members of a fraternity were asked to rate themselves and their fraternity brothers on a number of traits such as generosity, hostility, drive, laziness, honesty, reliability and narrowmindedness. The results were extraordinarily consistent: if Jones rated himself high on generosity, for instance, *and* if he rated most of his fraternity brothers as high in dishonesty, he himself in turn was rated by the majority of the others as rather dishonest and stingy. The moral of this story is that not only did he not want to realize his own shortcomings, but he indeed ascribed them to others. This phenomenon of "projection"—ascribing to others characteristics that one doesn't like in oneself—is a useful and not uncommon mechanism for trying to maintain one's own mental equilibrium. The Bible contains an understanding of this syndrome when it speaks of "beholding the mote in thy brother's eye and considering not the beam in thine own." (In fact, psychologist G. Ichheiser terms the tendency to criticize whole groups of the population—blacks, WASPs, Jews, Catholics or whatever—the "mote-beam mechanism"; especially when we find character traits in them which we do not want to acknowledge in ourselves.)

Another similar example of the defenses at work is the parent who gets drunk on his commuter train every evening but complains bitterly that his son is using drugs. Quick to deny his own alcoholism, to reject his own need for escape, he is apt to criticize it all the more vigorously in others.

These are examples of defense mechanisms misused. Yet many defenses are necessary for adaptation to life. For instance, the mechanism known as "repression" is an essential precursor of any sort of sophisticated society. We are in trouble indeed unless the individuals within a society learn the capacity to repress a good deal of aggression or sexuality. On the other hand, the boundaries are frequently not clear between genuine social defensiveness and simple prejudice. What, for example, of pornography? Is concern on this subject old-fashioned, or is there validity in the idea that too much erotic stimulation in too many books or movies may lead to unwarranted overstimulation, especially among the young? Indeed, the point could be made that our Western society is predicated upon a relatively controlled role for sexuality. Tropical isles, where one can go about exposed or, at will, repair to the nearest bush, may provide more in the way of sexual relaxation, but such cultures did not produce the industrial society. If technological developments are desirable, then it is obviously necessary to forego some immediate drive gratifications. The whole field of sexual license is clearly a fertile one for extensive discussion. What indeed is the value of defenses? What price does one pay for having them? What are the reasonable limits of defenses? When is it preferable for defenses to be established, or relaxed?

Neither a maximum of defensiveness nor a minimum of it is most adaptive. A minimum of defenses leaves us at the mercy of all our drives and impulses, from laziness to murderousness. A maximum of defensiveness makes us narrowminded, overly rigid, opinionated, intolerant and eventually paralyzed. Some rigid people, for example, can become so concerned about feeling dirty morally, sexually or otherwise, that they become overpreoccupied with cleanliness in different forms. The woman who has to wash each glass at least three times finds it difficult to get her other daily chores done. Her concern is, to say the least, unrealistic. At the same time, she may become a fanatic about ecology and pollution. Such defenses, however, are not always consistent with the apparent fervor they engender. As one poor husband complained, "Why does my wife's concern with pollution stop at her own front porch?" Apparently his wife was passionately concerned about the pollution of the environment but didn't show much solicitousness about the disorderliness of her own house.

Other types of defenses that prevent optimum functioning tend to be connected with guilt over "bad" feelings. One male patient I know of suffered from confusion, perplexity and depression. The perplexity and confusion were primarily defenses against the rage he felt toward his wife. A physical illness of hers imposed tremendous burdens upon him; he did not want to recognize his anger about this situation and chose instead to repress it. It resurfaced, however, as depression, as helplessness on his own part. It was as if he had said "I really can't help her; I feel helpless, perplexed, confused myself." His depression was an aspect of his attempt to deal with his anger; he thus turned it against himself rather than permitting the outward expression of it. In essence, he was saying that he felt he was a bad person for feeling that selfish.

An important problem of adaptation, then, is to not let oneself be carried away into excessive use of defenses *or* into too little use of them. People who live by the slogan "Black is (more) beautiful" are engaging in the same process of rationalization as those who always proclaimed white supremacy.

In the confusion of our rapidly changing society, man feels increasingly helpless to deal with his fate. Different peoples have employed different defensive measures to deal with that problem. Orientals, in the past, probably developed fatalism as a defense against the fact that their lives were miserable no matter which conqueror or warlord ruled them at one time or another. Disease and starvation seemed beyond their control. The *mañana* spirit of South Americans, on the other hand, may in part be the result of a fortunate environment of warmth and natural resources. To a certain extent, however, there is also a defensive fatalism involved, in that much of the South American economy has been so hopeless and the fate of the majority of the people so irreversible that they have lost reason for motivation. The same can be said for grossly underprivileged groups of any nation anywhere. It was Karl Marx who insisted that the poorest of the poor—the group he called the *lumpenproletariat*—could not be interested in revolution. Only skilled workers would have enough motivation left from their struggle for survival to want to change their lot.

In this country, the current revival of astrology and other manifestations of the occult represents an attempt to adapt to the feeling of being overwhelmed by our technology, overwhelmed by modern man's insignificance in relation to the computer and the atomic bomb, and by the incomprehensible changes in all the old landmarks by which we conducted our daily lives. If one's fate is fixed by being born under the sign of Aquarius, then one need not worry any more about what might happen. One's fate is in the stars, and it is all prescribed for better or for worse. To see a large modern kiosk in Grand Central Station in New York City serving up astrological pronouncements as devised by computers is indeed a farcical phenomenon of our times.

Drugs also deserve consideration as an attempt to defend against the cares of our lives. One martini before dinner or some wine with dinner may have some adaptive value in that it relieves some of the tensions accumulated in the course of the day and allows one to relate more pleasantly to the family. However, extensive use of alcohol, or the use of marijuana, heroin and other drugs to get away from either inner or outer turmoil is highly unadaptive, and leads to an increasing avoidance of all problems of adaptation or to an inability to cope with them. Chinese society, which was, prior to the present regime, highly dependent on opium is one frightening example of how drugs can affect the adaptiveness of a whole, huge population. Alcoholism is already the largest single social problem in America (there are 9,000,000 alcoholics out of 80,000,000 drinkers) and in much of Western society.

Proposed Remedies

If one can accept the fact that defenses, in their negative manifestation, are used for scapegoatism, prejudices, political polarization and stereotyped thinking, it is well to consider how to minimize this sort of distortion over the long range by bringing up children with a better tolerance for ambiguity. It must be possible for children to grow up with a better ability to think and act flexibly rather than concretely. Black/white, polarized thinking is the bane of intelligent judgment and has got to be abandoned. An attitude of increased tolerance for other people's viewpoints should lead to sounder, more workable solutions to complex interpersonal problems.

The educational system is probably here, again, the key. Almost every school subject can be taught in such a way that the student learns increasing tolerance, and, indeed, respect, for intellectual and emotional ambiguity. Instead of placing heavy emphasis on the historical rightness of "our side," young people will have to learn that major problems have more than one side, whether those problems have to do with individuals or with the international arena. Our children should be enabled to grasp abstractions and nuances of historical events rather than merely being taught "facts." If problems are reduced to a level basic enough (which they can be), even people of limited deductive capacity can be taught to conceptualize more than one side of a situation at a time.

Science, with its history of discovery through trial and error and its natural ability to supersede favored but erroneous doctrines, is an especially ideal vehicle for teaching the relativity of truth. Furthermore, it is unusually free of ideology, propagandizing and cant. The more exact the discipline, the less distracting and confusing its premises. At the same time, the lessons of irony, tolerance, surprise and reevaluation are not lost.

chapter 11

STIMULUS BARRIER
and the INPUT CRISIS

How do you feel when caught in crosstown traffic in the midst of a hundred cars blowing their horns, while overhead a plane breaks the sonic barrier and, because it is election time, soundtrucks blare out loud music intermingled with campaign slogans?

Modern life has meant a crescendo of input of all kinds of stimuli, not only sound. Crowding means, among other things, that more people have an impact on you with elbows, with words, with faces. It means that the telephone jangles your nerves, that bulk mail brings you much more than you can read, that radio, television, the movies, advertisements in the sky constantly assault you. If you go to a restaurant, the tables are too close together. The din is probably almost unbearable, privacy unattainable, and all this after having had to wait in line, particularly if it is a weekend. If you are unfortunate enough to have to ride a subway, you are affected not only by the thundering noise and by the fact that you are packed in like a sardine, but also by a large variety of smells, explosive tempers and the uncertainty of mechanical functioning.

Should you move to the suburbs? Chances are that, while you are trying to shave, probably to the noise of your electric razor, your neighbor has either his gasoline-driven lawnmower or snowblower in action, and one of the tree men is cutting down branches with an electric saw (you would have done as well in Dante's Inferno). Meanwhile, the radio assails you with ads enticing you to one of various tropical isles, in between the recounting of earthquakes in California, fighting in the Near East and the Far East, and about half a dozen strikes. If you can watch television at the same time, your stimulus input may also include a number of very scantily clad girls. For that matter, a great deal of sexual stimulation is more a part of the contemporary scene than it has been in a long time.

The body, and particularly the brain, has to do something with all these many effects. They have to be screened, suppressed, acted upon, organized, and it all takes energy. But at some point the brain's electrical system is unable to handle the overload. We know, for example, that convulsions can be produced in experimental animals if they are exposed to sound that is loud enough and high enough in intensity. In the case of humans, the effect of overloading can sometimes be very clearly observed. Sometimes a patient will appear whose symptoms of confusion, panic and perplexity are so intense that he is virtually unable to perform the tasks of day-to-day living. History-taking will show that these symptoms regularly occur at the most difficult times of day—in the early evening, for instance, when the children have come home, the dinner has to be prepared and a large amount of energy has been already used up during the day. This high level of input is likely to lead to trouble in a person whose barrier or threshold for stimuli is lower than others, or in a person who is regularly exposed to very high levels, such as the mother of young children. The result is a dysfunctioning, not dissimilar to certain forms of battle fatigue.

There are different ways of reacting to excessive impact. When there were still boilermakers, people had to live with the cacophony of constant hammering, and one occupational disease was boilermaker's deafness. Cilia in the inner ear, like the strings of some musical instruments, are of different lengths and respond to different frequencies of sound. In the case of the boilermaker, the sound organs corresponding to the frequency they were most exposed to simply deteriorated. They could not hear sound in that frequency range any more. We know that the same is true of artillery soldiers. Sound, light, touch and temperature may, however, also have a stimulating effect.

There is the incredible input, too, from the "psychedelic" phenomena and the inconceivably loud level of rock and roll music, both of which seem to excite (apparently pleasantly) the younger population, while driving the older one out of its mind. We often seem to be left with the Hobson's choice between feeling excessively stimulated or excessively dulled and blasé from the tremendous impact of all kinds of stimuli that flood our senses, body and mind. One's attitudes, political and personal, may fluctuate between apathy and immoderate responsiveness, especially anger. More "inputs" are crowded per unit into our lives than ever before.

PROPOSED REMEDIES

In a way, the input problem of our society resembles another input problem typical of our time, e.g., the possibility that radiation levels from television and other electronic machinery are excessive. As in many other fields, the answer to protection against the crisis of excessive input has to be both a governmental and a personal one. On the public level, an increasing amount of attention will have to be paid to attempts to hold down the noise level and other input. Measures in that direction include banning automobile hornblowing, controlling airplane noise and soundproofing factories.

Urban planning should include provisions to make sure that travel to and from work, for instance, is held to a minimum, and that traffic in general is decreased. (At least one community, Reston, Virginia, is laid out along such human lines.) Man in his personal life may have to more and more exercise the option *not* to take advantage of available means of entertainment, travel and other opportunities for stimulation. Cultivation of inner directedness rather than outer directedness may be indicated. The era of the frantic cocktail party may have to evolve into a social life of quieter relationships with fewer people. Every person may have to learn to arrange tranquil periods in his life away from the usually hectic interaction. Western interest in yoga and Zen Buddhism may be one indicator of the need felt by many for more internal peace and less barrage from the nearly unlimited possibilities of our modern society.

chapter 12

AUTONOMOUS FUNCTIONS

"Autonomous functions" is a rather fancy psychoanalytic term for those abilities that are innate, such as skillfulness in handling one's body, special mechanical skills, artistic ability and even, to a certain extent, intelligence and memory. The psychoanalysts call these functions "autonomous" to distinguish them from much everyday action which, they feel, is the result of conflicts between drives and conscience, between drives and reality. In other words, *primary* autonomous functions are those abilities one is born with and which are thus autonomous —that is, not the result of conflictual striving.

There are also *secondary* autonomous functions. An activity, for instance, might have had its origin in conflict, but have become entirely independent of it. A surgeon, for instance, might have started out with a desire to hurt animals or people, but his conscience keeps him from it. If this conflict is well resolved, he finds his satisfaction in the surgical activity which retains some of the original desire to do something destructive but in a way totally acceptable to his conscience and to society. He has put his original drive in the service of mankind, and it is now quite independent (autonomous) of the original evil wishes or the struggle with his conscience. Anyone with such a conflict who cannot resolve it to this point either suffers neurotic anxieties or is a danger to society as a sadist.

It is part of the adaptational crisis of our society that some of the innate skills of the average person are overtaxed. Another aspect of the crisis lies in the fact that our society makes the development of secondary autonomous functioning and pleasure therein (sometimes called sublimation or neutralization of drives) more difficult than in the past. For instance, skilled workmanship permits a cabinet-maker much more sublimation of aggressive drives into the prideful details of his craft than would be possible if he were doing automated factory work.

One example illustrating how ordinary innate skills are overtaxed is the act of driving an automobile. Driving involves eye-hand coordination and good reflexes. You have to be able to adjust the speed of the car to the prevailing traffic conditions, to be able to stop at a moment's notice, or swerve, or accelerate. It necessitates, in fact, a great deal of excellent body coordination, not to mention the ability to anticipate, to take the local traffic pattern into consideration and to keep looking back as well as to the side and front. High-speed driving in our high-powered automobiles takes, I suspect, on the basis of daily observation, more bodily coordination, motor skill and better reflexes than most people have available to them. I believe it is this basic fact that accounts for most of those car accidents that are not related to defective machinery, inadvertent conditions, or to alcohol. In some ways, it could be said that the technological development of society has outrun the bodily equipment of a large part of the population. The attention span of many people is overburdened by all the facts of modern life.

On the other hand, many bodily functions are simply not used any more. Walking has become a nearly unknown activity, and automation has done away with most of the need for the mechanical use of the body, thus interfering with an important method of decreasing tension. Also, the sense of fulfillment that was inherent in the simple physical labor required in the days before cars, planes, electrified kitchens and central heating took over is now absent. It is less trouble but it is also less satisfying to simply heat up a TV dinner than to prepare a good dinner. The same can be said for the role of the active production of most goods. Pride in craftsmanship, be it that of a butcher, or a carpenter, or a housepainter, has disappeared. The fact is that many of the crafts that were once of great importance and that are still playing some role in European society have for all practical purposes vanished from American life. Metal tooling, bookbinding, the repair of everyday articles, dressmaking, shoemaking, the production of fine jewelry have for the most part given way to machinery. The impersonalization inherent in mass production of goods is responsible for a certain amount of discontent or lack of pleasure in what one does. It is hard to take much pride in a product when one's role in its production consists of pressing several buttons or turning screws on an assembly line.

With the decrease of personalized pleasure in the exercise of one's skills goes also much less of a sense of commitment to the work. Work has much more plainly become merely a source of income. Clockwatching is the result of a failure to take pride and pleasure in one's work. Along with the loss of satisfaction in a job well done, comes a loss in the feeling of responsibility for it, and thus a loosening of one base for social ties. The workman has less interest in his product and therefore less concern for the consumer of his goods. In the mass market of mass products, obsolescence is not only planned in our economy, but is also the natural result of the worker's reduced interest in doing quality work.

In an indirect way, the decrease of enjoyment in doing things well has brought about a character change in the modern population. It has encouraged a desire to simply get by, to get it over with. This feeling has added a great deal to the sense of emptiness in our technical society. At the same time, the lack of a chance for a certain amount of energy discharge through labor in the field, in the smithy or the kitchen—indeed, the lack of the pleasure of *physical* fatigue—leaves modern man with a great deal of motor restlessness. Add the fact that after his sedentary day at work he is likely to return home to sit down in front of the TV, and we have indeed a creature whose chances of fighting off obesity are poor. The modern officeworker who steps from his apartment door into the elevator and from there into the bus, or his own car—or even a farmer who simply steps into his tractor—does not use his body enough to use up the amount of cholesterol from a couple of breakfast eggs, let alone the large dinner he is likely to eat. People are also increasingly vulnerable to afflictions of the muscular system, such as low back pain. Diseases of the vascular system—such as high blood pressure and coronary disease—are also encouraged because of insufficient exercise.

Too much of the average American's leisure time is spent watching sports rather than participating in them. And those sports that are played are getting "easier" all the time. The walking that used to be part of golf has usually been replaced now by golf carts. In fact, the whole country club scene involves more drinking and overeating than any athletic activity. If there is a pool, it is used more or less for esthetic display. Certainly there isn't enough exercise in an occasional ten yards of swimming. Tennis still calls for vigor, but even skiing has lost much of its athletic value due to technological developments. Now the snowmobile seems the ultimate development in taking the "sport" out of winter sports, and they are steadily gaining in popularity. In summer, power boats have taken the place of canoeing, rowing and sailing, and noisy motorcycles have replaced bicycles.

PROPOSED REMEDIES

To a certain extent we live in an adaptational crisis of bodily skills and of bodily activities that has been brought forth by the development of automation and mass production in our society. We have described elsewhere the fact that such autonomous functions as memory, anticipation and intelligence cannot quite keep up with the demands of our modern society.

We cannot go back, even with the help of a time machine, to again enjoy the exercise of skills that have now been lost, any more than we can do so in other areas of our culture. However, if our bodies are not to suffer increasingly from degenerative disease, especially in view of the otherwise longer life expectancy, it will be necessary to participate much more in regular athletics than is now customary. The Fitness Training Program sponsored by President Kennedy, a program executed through the schools to encourage the physical development of children, was one important step in that direction. Such programs will have to be extended through high school and college, and possibly made part of the routine of adults. In England it is apparently still much more customary than is the case on the American scene for adults to belong to a club that permits them to engage in a variety of sports.

chapter 13

SYNTHETIC FUNCTION

The synthetic function of the ego can be defined as the ability to reconcile incongruent attitudes and roles. One cannot integrate discrepant mental sets and rapidly changing roles when one is confused and often out of step, when part of one's personality is not functioning well. One feels estranged and out of tune with the times. It is hard to be able to behave adaptively in the face of swift social changes.

A famous French psychiatrist and contemporary of Freud's, Pierre Janet, in the early part of the century gave a good example of a failure of what we now call the synthetic function. He spoke of a typical French lady who went to market with her net bag. She tried to bring home as much as possible and filled that bag with cabbages, carrots, bread, tomatoes, rolls and potatoes. She was too ambitious and bought more than the net bag could hold. First some potatoes spilled out; and when she stuffed those back, some rolls fell out; a head of cabbage dropped out when she put the rolls back in. The net bag simply could not retain all that it was supposed to encompass.

The most dramatic psychiatric examples of failure of the synthetic function are the celebrated cases of split personalities. *The Three Faces of Eve* and *Dr. Jekyll and Mr. Hyde* are the most well known cases in literature. If a person has enough divergent desires, it is as if the synthetic function is not strong enough to contain them, to keep one suppressed or produce some healthy integration among them. Instead, "splitting" occurs so that the person acts like Jekyll at one time and Hyde at another. The major amnesias are another example of poor synthetic power. Part of an event is too painful for a person to accept and stay conscious of; thus he may forget who he is or where he is for various lengths of time.

A very absentminded person is a relatively mild example of failure of synthesis. It is as if he finds all the events in his life and all the stimuli around him too much to contain. Some people behave this way especially after the impact of serious upsets that absorb so much of their mental energy that they do not have enough left over to integrate the rest of their lives. Almost everyone has at some time or another found it difficult to concentrate or to perform certain tasks because some other event distracts his attention. A person in love invests so much into his love object and is so preoccupied with the loved one that his level of performance on the job, for instance, may be much decreased. His ability to synthesize the passion of his life with the necessary occupational roles he has to play is not strong enough to keep his synthetic function in good working order. The constant changes in our current society demand more absorption than ever, and the demand on our integrative capacity may be too great.

School integration and the busing of children are among the burdensome changes. A middle-aged Southerner today has to be able to reconcile the prejudices that have been inculcated from childhood with the changed status of blacks in today's society. Since all of us are in contact with many more people from different cultures, whether American cultures or cultures from other countries, our ability to accept different mental sets, different mores and different behavior patterns is more taxed than ever before.

For a while the synthetic function of university officials was paralyzed by student demands. It took them a period of time to psychologically reconcile student dissent with the traditional role of the trustees in such a way as to adaptively control irrational violence and, at the same time, to allow the students who were dissenting with intelligence to participate in the decision-making process. The synthetic function of parts of the community was overstrained by the shock induced by changing cultural and social roles among militant students and blacks; violence erupted, in essence, because the establishment was unable to adjust to these changes. Prejudice is, among other things, a failure to tolerate ambiguity. Tolerance of ambiguity involves the synthesizing function, the ability to integrate different viewpoints in such a way as to adapt rather than to give way to stereotyping or rather to allow one's beliefs to polarize to the point of paranoia.

Because socioeconomic patterns are changing so swiftly, many people are often burdened by the need to integrate discrepant roles they play. For instance, within a relatively short period, a person may move upward from poverty to affluence, from an underprivileged role to one of importance. This holds true, of course, mainly for the minorities—and most especially for the black minority.

Changes in sexual roles were originally largely brought about by scientific developments. The antibiotics made venereal disease less of a threat, and birth control pills made more casual sex possible. But since then there has been a vast change in sexual mores, making it possible for *Playboy* magazine to carry on earnest discussion by Masters and Johnson of the technicalities of anal intercourse. This seems a good example of how much change has to be absorbed these days. The mere idea of anal intercourse was once taboo for the overwhelming portion of the population. In fact, it was considered one aspect of sodomy. If a wife complained that her husband had such interests, even if he did not actively participate in them, it was almost certain that the court would decide a divorce in her favor. But nowadays, in the case of a complaint about such an interest or request by a spouse, it is very doubtful that any higher court would still automatically rule that way, given today's social climate. The emphasis here is on the attitudes of the *higher* court because it is entirely possible that a judge in a lower court would not have sufficient synthetic ability to absorb the social changes of our time. It is generally true that the higher courts are more sensitive and sophisticated about these changes; the members have more courage of their convictions, and judges of higher intellectual caliber usually have the better synthesizing capacity so as to, as it were, legislate changes, be it in labor relations, sexual relations or school integration. One could almost say that the major function of the Supreme Court is to exercise the synthetic function appropriate to integrate and reconcile differing attitudes and mores with the changes in the times, and embody them in a new interpretation of the law. The majority of people, for instance, and surely most lower courts, would have held that any school is entitled to start off its morning with a school prayer. It took the Supreme Court to find that to "inflict" such a practice on the student body offended the principle of separation of church and state. This ruling has proved a difficult fact of life to reconcile with the fundamentalist upbringing of many school board trustees or school principals throughout the country.

Adapting to new developments is a very important function. To be able to do so involves synthesis of new and old. Since there is more "new" to absorb in our current society than in any other, it follows that the synthetic function is more strained than ever. Considering all this, our society has not coped too badly so far as this particular ego function is concerned. In the last few years the failures of synthetic function have been relatively shortlived. The riots on campuses, the summer riots in the black ghettos and the response to them made by the constituted authorities were only relatively, and for a brief time, maladaptive; "brief" certainly not in terms of the tragedy at Kent State and in a number of southern communities, but brief in the terms of an historical overview. Instead of leading to a revolt by the Left, or a dictatorship by the Right, as such failures have in many countries, these events were reconciled in the United States surprisingly promptly. In turn, student radicals (for a while misled by groups such as SDS and the Weathermen) quickly came to realize that success was more likely to result from constructive activity. That does not mean that there is no more dissent or that militant students or blacks have disavowed their struggle. It simply means that they, too, have been able to exercise their synthetic function and behave more adaptively in the service of their ideas and needs.

PROPOSED REMEDIES

One area where integration of different roles and emotions is lagging is in international relations. Delegation of impulse control, of the drive to act aggressively, works much better within the context of city and nation than within the international world. In the broadest sense, that is what the problem of controlling war is about. Whether it is a question of a Marxist becoming warlike because of a drive for power and acquisition, or of a moralist who sees war as a means of protecting certain ideals, the fact is that both are capable of engaging in violence because they perceive no other means of obtaining their goals. Extreme and rigid doctrines cause impulsive behavior.

Surely the urge to wage war also has much to do with national vested interests, great complexity of issues and long-established alliances and bitternesses; but in essence, war is an overall failure to synthesize differing emotional and intellectual forces.

chapter 14

MASTERY-COMPETENCE

A person's sense of mastery and competence has been defined as his ability to perform in relation to his existing capacity, that is, his ability to interact with, and to master, the world around him. One's sense of competence derives from the degree to which one has lived up to one's own expectations of success.

As in the case of so many other ego functions, our contemporary world makes it very difficult to maintain a sense of competence and mastery. It is indeed hard to feel the master of circumstances that constantly change and that produce an abundance of developments that seem to be entirely beyond our control.

The psychological state of today's man is marvelously exemplified by the old story of the "Sorcerer's Apprentice." In this famous ballad of Goethe's, *Der Zauberlehrling*, the apprentice tries his hand at sorcery during the master's absence. Before too long, he is entrapped by the creatures he has conjured. The chaotic activities of a broomstick magically turned robot threaten his very existence. We, too, in our society, became sorcerers' apprentices by unleashing atomic power and by developing polystyrenes and the other plastics that threaten to engulf us.

Some political issues are too complex for most of us to feel competent to deal with. Contemporary man has more reason to feel insignificant now than he has for many generations. The role of the individual has been greatly decreased; a person frequently feels that he is little more than the smallest cog in a machine that is too large. One's actions are increasingly controlled by the federal, centralized authority —understandably so, because the community is so tightly interdependent that almost anything anyone does or might do could drastically affect its stability. Political control has increased to a certain extent because political treason could so easily upset a delicate balance of power. Arms control has to be stricter because arms are much more efficient than ever before. Environmental protection, and therefore restrictions, are essential because the possible dangers have so vastly increased. In view of these facts, the individual role and individual freedom have been severely limited. This may be for the common good, but certainly the individual's sense of mastery and competence is much diminished.

Existentialism in its literary and philosophical forms has been most successful in catching modern man's lack of feeling of mastery and competence.

Such writers as Sartre and Camus are primarily concerned with the basic helplessness of man. George Orwell in his chilling projection of the future, *1984*, diagrammed man's loss of individual creativity and control in a super-organized society. Even when it was published, many years ago now, *1984* caused a shock of recognition in its readers. Today, with egregious cases of wiretapping and military surveillance in the headlines, it is difficult to escape the actual prophetic quality of Orwell's imagination.

PROPOSED REMEDIES

To a certain extent, the feeling of loss and lack of mastery and competence will decrease as we eventually integrate the many new developments of our world. The new generation growing up may be developing a character structure sufficiently different so as to handle the continued rapid changes in our society even more smoothly than the current generation, which still carries a nucleus of the attitudes of older generations. These young people may feel less overwhelmed by rapid change or vast control systems.

In an attempt to restore the individual's sense of mastery and competence, it will be necessary to restore to the individual as many functions as is possible in a modern superstate. This is essential in order to increase the individual's willingness to participate responsibly in the affairs of state—so necessary for the survival of a healthy body politic.

chapter 15

GUIDELINES for CHANGE

Within each chapter, I have suggested remedies for the adaptive problems pertaining to the various ego functions. The remedies, which deserve particular and careful consideration, are distinguishable from one another, and at the same time are largely interdependent. A brief summary of some of the main proposals is offered here:

In our society of rapid technological change, nearly all values shift equally fast. That which was unattainable yesterday, whether economically or technologically, is commonplace and devalued today. Travel, sexual mores, religious standards, clothing, art and the stock market change so quickly and profoundly that we are often left overloaded, confused and disoriented. Important landmarks, such as familiar streets, are speedily altered. Buildings are razed and rebuilt almost overnight; friends and relatives move constantly. Modern corporate habit and policy relocate thousands of families anywhere in the world.

But there are positive aspects to our society of rapid technological change: most of us are better off financially, better informed about events and are given greater opportunities to lead the legendary "good life" than was true for previous generations.

Still, these changes occasionally have a dizzying effect on adults and perhaps even more so on children. While they are growing and trying to acquire an orientation to the world, children need some well-defined guidelines. They want to know who is stronger, the lion or the elephant; who is richer, Howard Hughes or Nelson Rockefeller. By establishing some order in the universe they create landmarks and establish guidelines for themselves.

Some regulators can be internalized: for instance, whereas the body temperature of so-called "cold-blooded" animals varies with the outside temperature, "warm-blooded" animals have a self-regulatory mechanism like a built-in thermostat. Within a small range of variation, the latter's body temperature stays the same independent of external conditions. Similarly, if one's internal values, such as honesty with oneself, are well-established, one is not at the constant mercy of outside opinions and alien values.

The adaptational crisis of our society can be considered analogous to the aggravated crisis that frequently occurs during the period of adolescence. Adolescents are generally quite upset by all the changes they go through. Physical and endocrine growth, the emergence of secondary sex characteristics, psychological and emotional adjustments—all are factors characteristic of this stage of development. Like the adolescent during this time of identity crisis, our society (and particularly our younger generation) has a wide-eyed approach to reality combined with openmindedness, a healthy spirit of criticism and a certain degree of naiveté. Our society has a hard time coping with its growing pains. Certainly the feelings of perplexity and helplessness that are so pervasive indicate that the severity of this critical period is equal to the severe crisis, characterized by seeming psychosis, that some adolescents who are badly in need of treatment suffer through.

Awareness of what is happening to us and to our children is the first step toward remedying the situation. Knowing that you are on a roller coaster goes a long way toward helping you adjust to it; you shift your weight, hold your breath, brace against it or swing with it. It is likewise important to understand the processes of change that affect us and the lives of our children. We must learn to minimize the destructive effects, the encroachment of the "machine," while enjoying the opportunities that proper use of the machine gives us for more time for leisure, travel, a higher standard of living. It helps to know that you or I are not the only ones affected, but everybody. This disorientation is happening not only in America but everywhere; German, Japanese, French and Italian parents and children are equally troubled by some of the changes that are going on worldwide; they, too, are drawn into a confusing period of crisis.

As with any doctor's treatment plan for a single patient, I believe we must think in terms of both *short-range* and *long-range* measures for society. Short-range treatment of social crisis is best considered in terms of "crisis intervention"—a course of action designed to deal with the acute stresses caused by overwhelming problems in contemporary society. In principle, crisis intervention can address itself to the alleviation of the circumstances leading to stress, and to the alteration of some of the ways in which individuals and the society adapt to the precipitating factors. To be effective, crisis intervention has to be prompt, concrete and skillfully applied.

If my diagnosis is correct—namely, that our society suffers significant anxiety caused by an unprecedented rate of change and excessive input, and that it therefore employs various maladaptive methods in attempting to deal with this anxiety—then I believe that we must all address our efforts toward crisis intervention. We cannot bring back yesterday or destroy the machines. We can, however, coordinate technology with "humanology." We can give consideration to the peripheral effects of what we do with things, rather than merely making and building them because we are able to.

In an article for *The New Yorker,* Lewis Mumford wrote:

> Not merely does technology claim priority in human affairs; it places the demand for constant technological change above any considerations of its own efficiency, its own continuity, or even, ironically, its own capacity to survive. . . . Many contemporaries are already so conditioned to accepting that technological "progress" is abso-

lute and irresistible—however painful, ugly,
mentally cramping, or physiologically damag-
ing its results—that they likewise accept the
latest technical offering ... with smiling con-
sent.

Even worse, the implications of many technical
and political innovations are rarely explored *before*
they are implemented, resulting, sometimes, in serious harm. This applies, for instance, to the mindless
and greedy manufacture of items from faulty toys to
fatal drugs, from dangerous automobiles to potentially destructive aircraft (such as the SST). It can
even apply to the nomination of totally unfit and
irresponsible persons to the Supreme Court of the
United States. In other words, time is not taken in our
headlong-dashing society to evaluate the possible effects of "progress" on the survival, not only
of individuals and communities, but of the planet
as well.

Short-Range Measures

I suggest that we need a Social Science Board,
comparable in its voluntary structure and independence to the Council on Foreign Relations. The social sciences, including psychiatry, are the *survival
sciences.* Alvin Toffler and Milton Katz have
proposed a technology board, but I see the need for
a broader structure, of which a technology board
would be only one part. A board of scientists, which
would include the broad viewpoint of all aspects of

the social sciences, would give careful consideration to the implementation of future technological developments. This new board could conceivably evolve into a body similar to the President's Council of Economic Advisors and eventually into a Federal Social Science Board or Social Science Commission.

As the world shrinks, international interactions increase. A world body such as the United Nations also needs a Social Science Commission as one of its potentially most important substructures. Such a regulatory body could, in the long run, do more to open a debate about the urge to wage war as a maladaptive behavior pattern than any other forum has so far done. Clearly, however, the details and the merits of such a commission, and its precise responsibilities, would have to be publicly debated at the UN, and carefully spelled out so as to convince the public that a moral *and* psychological equivalent of war was actually possible.

We need a national and international *Adaptation Register.* Just as the Gross National Product, unemployment statistics, and the consumer price index are indicators of the state of the national economy, indices of adaptation for regions, nations, and the entire world population are necessary. Local, national and international polls designed to evaluate the 12 ego functions would be one way of obtaining adaptive measures. We need to know the emotional temperature of college campuses, mill towns, the industrial areas of the Midwest and the agrarian South, for example, to evaluate the state of our nation. We must know what the problems of impulse control are in Detroit and what the problems of reality testing are in Kansas City. Ratings for each of the 12 variables for each of the 50 states would be very valuable to social scientists, although admittedly difficult to establish.

The problem of collecting data is, however, not as insurmountable as one might think. One easy way to begin this adaptive pulsetaking might be to study local newspapers for adaptive ratings. For a broader view of the nation and of the world, the summary provided by the Sunday *New York Times* could be rated for ego functions. It is likely that these weekly news summaries would provide an excellent idea of the state of the country and the world. Comparisons from week to week, month to month and year to year will provide surprisingly succinct data.

A reliable (and also more involved) method of gathering data for assessment of problems and adaptation would be to have groups consisting of citizens —perhaps college students interested in research— and a variety of scientists in many different places who would serve as local collectors of data on a large variety of social problems and forward them to regional centers which would in turn advise and report to a central governmental body such as the Social Science Commission.

By this means, responsible government, informed by, responsive to and in the final analysis represented by local authority, would be able to keep a hand on the emotional pulse of the country. Remedies for local problems would, as much as possible, remain in the hands of local people.

To many people, these measures may sound uncomfortably like Big Brother and thought control. To this, one can only reply that, regrettably, more interaction calls for more regulation.

The plan suggested for adaptation control has many forerunners and models which fulfill part of the need for adaptation and control of crisis. A net of public health stations and communicable disease centers is one of them. Regional collections of economic indicators, of weather and pollution observation and control are others. Certainly regulation of manufacturing processes and disposal of waste is neither more important nor less invasive than collection of data and control of emotional and other adaptational hazards in each community. The rise of Neofascism in Italy is an interesting example of the interaction of economic and emotional adaptational problems, as is particularly evident in such deprived regions as Sicily. Armored cars seem a very primitive way of dealing with an emotional crisis.

The crisis of American cities would especially profit from a broadly based adaptational study that would include regular reporting and quick measures, where possible, to avoid riots. Action research for combating prejudice as described, for instance, by Isadore Chein of New York University, John Harding of Cornell and others may be one of the useful models. They actually formulated manuals for questions and answers concerning problems of prejudice met with in everyday life. Economic crash programs of limited scope might be a parallel measure.

Our democratic process must be more realistically defined, away from the outmoded Greek city-state market place model; away from the ideal of the New England town hall meeting, which is no longer functional for our unwieldly social structure.

To make the democratic process meaningful, vital issues must be made understandable on a sixth grade level, which is a realistic way of dealing with the fact that 67 percent of the population has an IQ of 90–110. Professionals with excellent educations can hardly be expected to understand the details of the ABM or Federal Reserve policies unless that is their particular discipline or interest, or unless such matters are broken down to a fairly simple, easily digestible level; the professional has had no more training in these areas than the man on the street and is not automatically qualified to make judgments on such matters simply because he holds a degree.

Presentation of political news should be completely restyled. We cannot afford the confusion in reality testing that is an integral part of the time-honored political doubletalk. I am not speaking of idealistic notions of truth, but rather about basic necessities for survival. If any form of democracy is to survive, the voter has to be in a position to decide on the true merits of any candidate or issue before him. British politics has survived on drier stuff than American hoopla; it must be possible to separate fact from fiction more clearly, as John Gardner's Common Cause professes it will do. A news medium which might be sponsored by Common Cause and should be comparable to the *Consumer Reports* might carefully test news and political statements for truth content.

Better reality testing must be facilitated; the personalities of our politicians must be played down, and there should be no television blitzes by wealthy candidates. I would suggest that prepared position papers be read by professional speakers for all political sides. If information is properly organized and reasonably presented, television could well become a town hall meeting of the air. Eventually, it might be possible for the television audience to register its reactions to the issues presented at these meetings.

I further propose that candidates for high office be prescreened and evaluated for their physical and emotional fitness, even before they are nominated for office. One must be trained and licensed in order to become a plumber or electrician. Up till now, anyone—whether qualified or not—could run for an elective position. Some basic standards of competence and intelligence must be established and met by would-be candidates. Who would deny how important it is, especially in our time, that our presidents, senators and congressmen be emotionally stable and physically sound? Large corporations would not dream of selecting executives without some careful screening! People with poor impulse control, pathological indecisiveness or character disorders are obviously poor material for our most important elective positions. It is high time a bipartisan "jury" of qualified medical and psychological specialists carefully examined each prospective candidate and issued an *opinion* on his physical and mental health. Lest this idea upset anyone, let me remind you that it has long been customary for the Bar Association to make recommendations concerning prospective judicial candidates. The matter of professional judgment is not so foreboding if one keeps in mind that I do not propose that they *select* the best possible candidates, but merely that they keep the psychologically dangerously unfit persons out of contention.

Finally, a body of crisis intervention specialists should be available—like a fire brigade—to intervene quickly on the scene of a social crisis. Economists, psychologists, sociologists and others would have to collaborate on such Crisis Intervention Boards. There is at present some modest body of expertise in psychological and psychiatric crisis intervention. There are measures of emergency economic pump priming or other modifications and we have medical specialists for intervention in epidemics. The Red Cross is experienced in handling a wide variety of catastrophes.

Crisis intervention boards will have to incorporate all this knowhow and add a great deal of theoretical formulation as well as practical experience for dealing with such many-faceted human problems as the wage-price spiral, strikes, riots, lunatic fringe groups, drug addiction, alcoholism and the crime rate. To treat any of these problems only unidimensionally, either from the standpoint of money or of law and order—or for that matter, only from a psychological viewpoint—is ridiculous.

Until now we have engaged in piecemeal and uncoordinated, haphazard and shortsighted approaches to crisis. We can afford such luxury less every day.

LONG-RANGE MEASURES

Our society will not become simpler with time. Therefore, measures must be taken to ensure survival. Long-range goals geared to treatment of our society's ills are in many ways identical to the goals of prevention of future physical and mental ills in the individual. Clearly the treatment must be fitted to the malady.

If complexity is an outstanding trait of our world, steps must be taken to make it easier to deal with. To the extent to which the complexities are intellectual, our children—tomorrow's world citizens—have to be equipped to deal with them. Our task is to develop in them the basic ability to make valid inferences and form sound judgments. Our schools, for one, too often encourage rote learning of facts, rather than teaching students how to use information. Emphasis must be placed on teaching the student how to think. Too often he may go all the way through to the graduate level of study where he is taught the "scientific method," before he is taught the value of careful thinking and good judgment. Fancy as the "scientific method" sounds, this term implies nothing more than the process of cautiously drawing inferences based on sound assumptions. The student has to be acquainted with and made consciously aware of the process of making these inferences with the help of practical examples from the sciences, from history and from daily life. He has to learn the basic nature of the syllogism and be given many instances of past errors of judgment. The history of experimentation lends itself to this as well as the history of nations.

Abercrombie's admirable little book, *The Anatomy of Judgment,* clearly sets forth the basic principles of making judgments. Her discussion of the selective and interpretive nature of perception can show students how information is organized and how they can reinterpret and reorganize it to make it more meaningful. I myself have taught sixth graders in the local school system to make inferences, using the title, *Why We Behave the Way We Do.*

The most complex scientific procedure demands no more than that any inferences be based as carefully as possible on available facts, without jumping to conclusions that are unsubstantiated. The battle over the effects of cigarette smoking, for instance, could be discussed in any elementary school as an example of drawing a conclusion from carefully tested inferences. Some scientists claim that cigarette smoking causes lung cancer; others say that air pollution is probably responsible for the disease. Several checks were made: one was to have smokers and nonsmokers, who both breathed the same polluted city air, compared for frequency of lung cancer. It was found that cigarette smokers had a higher rate of lung cancer. Another check was made comparing smokers and nonsmokers in a rural area. In this case, also, smokers had lung cancer more frequently. More checks were made, all leading to the same conclusion: smoking plays a crucial role in relation to lung cancer. Thus it appears a valid inference on the basis of currently available facts.

Our children must also be taught to be increasingly tolerant of ambiguity. If hellfire and brimstone religious doctrines produced black and white approaches and intolerance of ambiguity, conversely it should be entirely possible to bring up children to tolerate ambiguity and to be able to think and act flexibly on racial, religious, political and economic issues.

For the past several years I have been urging that *children be screened for severe psychological problems upon entering school.* They are carefully examined for signs of physical illness; why not check for signs of mental disturbance as well? Where emotional disorders are found, remedial measures must be recommended and enforced. From my years of experience at the Troubleshooting Clinic, I have discovered that it does not require such extraordinary circumstances to produce a significant behavioral change without extended psychoanalysis. For instance, a father brought his young son to the Clinic one day with the complaint of recurring nightmares. It became known during the conversation that the child's aunt had recently come to live with them and had taken over his room; the child was now sleeping in the same bed with his parents. Instead of going into Oedipal research, I suggested the boy would be better off sleeping on a mattress on the floor in another room. The nightmares disappeared immediately when he moved into the kitchen.

Parents should also be offered help, or even forced to accept some form of treatment, if they are unable to cope adequately. It is ridiculous to assume that every couple who can conceive a child is fit to be good parents. Prospective spouses should not only be obliged to have negative Wasserman Test results, but also to show a fundamental knowledge of the growth and upbringing of children. It would be better from the preventative point of view if we could insist on their being in good mental health before they even had a child.

Long ago I suggested that there be a School for Parents. Groups of 10 to 12 parents of children at similar stages of development, with a trained advisor, would meet to discuss problems they faced with their children. The function of these groups would be twofold: one function would be to impart information— a mixture of Gesell, Piaget, Freud and Spock. Parents should know, for example, that eight-month-old infants may suddenly start to scream when they see a stranger. This is a sign of normal development; they have just learned to differentiate the mother from other people. The other function of the parent school should be to allow a forum for group discussion about problems; problems that trouble the parents themselves as well as problems concerning children. Parents with more serious problems could then be singled out for individual attention.

CONCLUSION

A rational approach to problem solving exists. One does one's best to understand or diagnose the problem and then tries to find and implement the most appropriate way of dealing with it.

This is the method suggested here for dealing with the many crises of our society.

If some of our society's ills resemble the adolescent crisis, there is also hope that a healthy resolution of the crisis, with the help of skilled intervention, may result. We should be able to achieve a maturation that leaves us, as a society, in a state *much better suited* not only to deal with rapid change, but better able to enjoy life generally. It is to the end of this common cause that we must work.

chapter 16

PROGNOSIS

During the past year our society has shown some upward trend in some of the ego functions—most notably, reality testing, judgment and impulse control. Constituted authority, as well as the public at large, seems to have gained a better understanding of some of the problems of everyday life, of integration, the role of youth and the emotional schism caused by Vietnam. The incidence of violence by student and black groups and by white vigilantes has much decreased.

In the short run, it is extremely likely that society's adaptational function will show marked fluctuations. Even when there is a turn toward the better, national and international situations need careful study and occasional crisis intervention to avoid dire results. I see as a bare minimum the equivalent of what in medical terminology we call "supportive treatment": that is, keeping the patient warm, supplied with fluids and at least permitting optimal conditions in which his own recuperative abilities can operate, if one cannot engage in more specific therapeutic actions. This latter course, of course, can be followed in many medical situations. It can also be done, as suggested before, for many of the social conditions under discussion.

For the long run, I predict that the adaptational curve with regard to most of the ego functions will be very similar to any learning curve. There will be some improvement, some leveling off, some occasional dipping, but the long-range trend has an excellent chance of being a very good one. Adaptation of any kind is a form of learning. Unless catastrophic conditions are permitted to interfere, it is very likely that the crisis of our society will be met by adaptation which will not only restore the conditions that existed before the crisis, but will lead to higher levels of integration and better forms of adaptation to the world than heretofore.

It does not appear likely that such an improvement of adaptation will be uniform. It seems difficult to believe at this moment in history that an individual's *sense of self* will indeed be restored to what it was before the current phase of rapid and extensive changes. Nor is it likely that *social relations* will recover the intensity, durability and depth that they once had. They may well be, however, more benign and more cosmopolitan than they have been and, in the long run, offer less chance for interpersonal friction on the individual or international level.

The sense of mastery and competence may also continue to decrease in the mechanized, controlled civilization of the future. It is possible that the collective social ability to control the environment may give the future generation a substitute for personal mastery.

At any rate, future generations are unlikely to be subjectively aware of these changes in their personality. We are not aware, for instance, of our greater sensitivity to cruelty than the contemporaries of Casanova who watched public torture and execution with relish.

Most of the younger generation, on the other hand, is not aware of missing something that they never had: the relative leisure of pre-World War II days, the greater social stability of the pre-World War I era in middle-class Europe or the personal satisfaction that quality performance could bring.

With the possible exception of these three "victims" of our social and technological changes—sense of self, sense of mastery and stability and depth of personal relations—the future is bright enough if we fight for it.

SELECTED REFERENCES

Preface

Bellak, Leopold, Hurvich, Marvin, and Gediman, Helen K. *Ego Functions in Schizophrenics, Neurotics and Normals.* New York: John Wiley & Sons, 1973.

Chapter 1

Wicker, Tom. In the nation: seeding the clouds. *The New York Times.* December 18, 1969.
Chapin, Emerson. The generation gap in Japan is almost an abyss. *The New York Times.* December 1, 1968.

Chapter 2

Hollingshead, A. B., and Rogler, Lloyd H. *Trapped: Families and Schizophrenia.* New York: John Wiley & Sons, 1965.

Lindemann, Erich. Symptomatology and management of acute grief. *American Journal of Psychiatry.* Vol. 101, September 1944.

Erikson, Erik. *Childhood and Society.* New York: W. W. Norton & Company, 1950.

Fromm, Erich. *Escape from Freedom.* New York: Holt, Rinehart & Winston, 1941.

Speer, Albert. *Inside the Third Reich.* New York: Macmillan Publishing Company, 1970.

Tuchman, Barbara. *The Proud Tower.* New York: Macmillan Publishing Company, 1966.

Barnett, John. Price of success? Growing job demands shatter the marriages of more executives. *The Wall Street Journal.* May 10, 1967.

Riesman, David. *The Lonely Crowd.* New Haven: Yale University Press, 1950.

Laqueur, Walter. A look back at the Weimar Republic—the cry was "Down with Das System." *The New York Times Magazine.* August 16, 1970.

Silberman, Charles E. *Crisis in the Classroom.* New York: Random House, 1970.

Caplan, Gerald. *Approaches to Community Mental Health.* New York: Grune & Stratton, 1961.

Chapter 3

Witcover, Jules. *The Resurrection of Richard Nixon.* New York: G. P. Putnam's Sons, 1970.

Packard, Vance. *The Wastemakers.* New York: David McKay Company, 1960.

McGinniss, Joe. *The Selling of the President 1968.* New York: Trident Press, 1969.

Chapter 4

Abercrombie, M. L. G. *The Anatomy of Judgment: An Investigation into the Processes of Perception and Reasoning.* New York: Basic Books, 1960.

Chapter 5

von Däniken, Erich. *Chariots of the Gods? Unsolved Mysteries of the Past.* New York: G. P. Putnam's Sons, 1970.
Erikson, Erik. *Identity, Youth and Crisis.* New York: W. W. Norton & Company, 1968.

Chapter 6

Galbraith, John Kenneth. *The Affluent Society.* Boston: Houghton Mifflin Company, 1969.

Chapter 7

Bellak, Leopold. Personality structure in a changing world. *Archives of General Psychiatry.* Vol. 5, August 1961.

Chapter 8

Köhler, Wolfgang. *The Mentality of Apes.* 2nd ed. New York: Random House, 1959.
Halberstam, David. *Making of a Quagmire.* New York: Random House, 1965.

Chapter 10

Ichheiser, G. Projection and the mote-beam mechanism. *Journal of Abnormal Social Psychology.* Vol. 42, 1947.

Chapter 15

Toffler, Alvin. *Future Shock.* New York: Random House, 1970.
Katz, Milton. Topics: the environment and "Technology Assessment." *The New York Times.* August 15, 1970.
Bellak, Leopold. *The Porcupine Dilemma.* New York: Citadel Press, 1970.

INDEX

Depressive reaction, case study of, 31-32
Derealization, 100, 102
Der Zauberlehrling, 181
Detour behavior, 137
   need for, 22
Detour thinking, eggheads and, 18
Differences, acceptance of, vs. hatred, 119
   See also Ambiguity, tolerance of
Discrimination, and reality testing, 94
Disorientation, as worldwide condition, 187
Dr. Jekyll and Mr. Hyde, 174
Documents, primary, and diagnostic inferences, 96
Domagk, G. K., 147
Double bind, 85, 143
Doubletalk, and public judgment, 81
Doublethink, 64
Doubt, reasonable, as characteristic of egghead, 17-18
Dreamers, eggheads considered as, 18
Dreams
   interpretation of, 141
   and reality testing, 57-58
Dreiser, Theodore, 40, 149
Drives
   neutralization of. *See* Autonomous functions
   regulation and control of, 111-20
      as ego function, 51
      proposed remedies for problems in, 118-20
Driving, and overtaxing of innate skills, 168-69
Dropping-out, as reaction to overload, 20-22
Drugs, and speed of perception, 61

Drug scene, as symptom of social unrest, 122
Drug use
   as defense mechanism, 158
   as escape from reality, 72, 124

Eastern cultures, apathy and fatalism in, 61
Economic situation(s)
   judgment of, 79
   vs. technological development, as major social concern, 6-7
Educational crisis, lack of synthesis in, reflected in art, 150
Eggheads, defined, 15
Ego, as man's adaptive mechanism, 49
Ego functions
   applied to study of society, 53
   listed, 50-52
   rating of, 50, 52, 190-91
   and rating of political candidates, 94-97
   studies of, 45-46, 50-56
Eisenhower era, and American society, 46
Elections, and exercise of judgment, 88-89
Emotion, vs. judgment, 82-83, 88
Emotional disorders, early detection of, 198
Emotional illness, 31-32
Emotional overload, defense against, 28
Emotional state, of society, need for gauge of, 119
Encounter groups, 128-29
Erikson, Erik, 35, 106, 206, 207
Escape from Freedom, 36
Escape, lack of, 27
Europeans, and creativity, 146-47
Everest syndrome, 28

Executive wives, effects of
mobility on, 37
Existentialism
and problems of identity,
100
reflecting lack of mastery and
competence, 182-83
Extremists, social, compared
to schizophrenics, 82

Facts
distortion of, effect on reality
perception, 61-62
techniques of ascertaining, 90
Family life, togetherness in, 128
Family, nuclear, 130-31
Farrell, James T., 149
Fashion, and homosexual influence, 150-51
Fatalism
danger of, 23
as defense mechanism, 157
Father, learning of role of, 125
Fear, and destructive behavior,
116
Feininger, Andreas, 149
Feudal Age, end of, and chang-
ing values, 40
Fitness Training Program, 172
Fitzgerald, Zelda and Scott,
as typical of twenties, 40
Fluoridation issue
and need for reality testing,
74
paranoid reactions to, 83
Fluorocarbons, and destruction
of ozone layer, 24-25
Food additives, and problems
of judgment, 84
Food and drugs, and emotion
vs. judgment, 83
Food, contamination of, 24
Ford, Gerald, 79
Forrestal, James, suicide of, 88
Frankness, disadvantages of,
127

Freedom, threats to, 25-26
Freud, Sigmund, monograph
on discontent, 72
Fromm, Erich, 36, 206
Frustration tolerance
and modern youth, 115
as task in childrearing, 119
Functioning, adaptive, in relation to environment, 46
See also Adaptation; Adaptive
functions; Adaptive re-
sponses
Future, prognosis for society,
201-3
"Future shock," 6

Galbraith, John Kenneth, 207
Gardner, John W., 43, 91, 193
Gediman, Helen K., 205
Generals (military), eggheads
vs. squareheads as, 17
Generation, changing time span
of, 39-40
German society, adaptive fail-
ures of, 36
Goebbels, Joseph Paul, propa-
ganda techniques of, 81
Goethe, Johann Wolfgang, 181
influenced by Rousseau, 20
Goldwater, Barry, 97
Good, varying meanings of, 16
Government
and distortion of reality, 65-68
and emotional pulse of
country, 191
intervention in emotional
crises (of society), 120
Grief reactions, normal and
pathological, 34-35
Groups, behavior of, 37

Halberstam, David, 139, 207
Haldeman, H. R., character of,
19
Harding, John, 192

Hartmann, Heinz, 45
Hauptmann, Gerhard, 149
H-bomb threat, and modern
    youth, 115
Heller, Joseph, 104
Helplessness, universal, 23
Herzog, 149
Heyderdahl, Thor, 81
Hippie movement
    as example of superficial rela-
        tionships, 122
    and identity crisis, 104-5
Hitler, Adolf, and misguiding
    of public, 81
Hoffman, Judge, and the
    Chicago Seven, 116
Hollingshead, A. B., 34, 205
Homosexuals, role in the arts,
    150-51
Human contact, as necessity in
    medical care, 130
Humaneness, impersonalized,
    122
"Humanology"
    coordinated with technology,
        188
    need for experts in, 73-74
Human relations, superficial, as
    defense, 28
Humor, sense of, eggheads vs.
    squareheads, 18
Hurvich, Marvin, 205
Husserl, Edmund, 100

Ibsen, Henrik, 149
Ichheiser, G., 154, 208
Identity crisis, 99-106
    proposed remedies, 106-9
Identity feelings, and familiar
    surroundings, 128
Illegitimacy, changing attitudes
    to, 40
Illness, acute, as adaptive crisis,
    12-13
Impact, excessive, reactions to,
    163

Impermanence, vs. permanence,
    as key to modern society,
    103
Impersonalization
    as characteristic of modern
        age, 104
    and mass production, 169-70
Improvisation, creative, 145
Impulse control, and judgment,
    93, 94
Industrial Revolution, and
    changing values, 40
Individual(s)
    decreased role of, 182-183
    psychiatric study of, applica-
        tion of, to problems of
        society, 55
    restoration of functions to,
        183
Individualism, and fringe bene-
    fits, 38
Individuality, feeling of, as
    component of sense of
    reality, 100
Inferences, valid, based on
    facts, 197
Inflation, 39
Informational overload, 28
    and reality distortion, 70
    and school children, 44
    See also Information explo-
        sion
Information, conflicting, and
    crisis from overload, 11
Information explosion, 135-36
    and attention overload, 140
Inner directedness, vs. outer
    directedness, as stimulus
    control, 165
Input crisis, 161-65
    proposed remedies for, 164-
        65
Integration, school, 175
Interaction, social, producing
    tension, 112
Interdependence, and need for
    controls, 182, 192

(Relationships . . . cont.)
See also Human relations; Interpersonal relationships
Religious dogma, influence on judgment, 85-86
Religious systems, squareheads as products of, 16-17
Repression, as defense mechanism, 155
Resource mobilization, as third phase of crisis, 47
Restlessness, and lack of physical labor, 170
Reston, James, 87
Reston, Virginia, 164
Resurrection of Richard Nixon, 63
"Retrieval system" crisis, 135
Riesman, David, 41, 206
Right, the, emotional reactions of, 64
Rigidity, of squareheads, 15-16
Robespierre, Maximilien F.M.I. de, influenced by Rousseau, 20
Rock and roll music, effects of, 163-64
Roentgen, Konrad, 138
Rogler, Lloyd H., 205
Rokeach, M., open and closed mind, concept of, 16
Role changes, and identity feelings, 102
Role identity, and fashion, 151
Role-playing, 124-26
Roles
changing conventions and, 125
integration of, 173
public vs. private, 126
Roman Empire, decline and fall of, 35-36, 40
Romanticists, influenced by Rousseau, 20
Rorschach test, in reality testing, 69, 70, 71
Roth, Philip, 147, 149

"Rousseau Delusion," 20-22
Rousseau, Jean Jacques, as forerunner of social dropouts, 20
Ruesch, J., 143

Sanity, ways of retention of, 108
Sartre, Jean-Paul, 100, 183
Scapegoat idea, avoidance in child-rearing, 119
Scapegoats, 117
Schizophrenia
depersonalization and derealization in, 100
thought disorder in, 143
Schizophrenic behavior, and double bind, 85
Schizophrenic(s)
adaptive problems of, 50
catatonic, 121
emotional reactions of, 64
feelings of, 105
School for Parents, proposed, 199
School life, and feeling of impermanence, 103
School prayer issue, 177
Schools
and increased tolerance, 159
and judgmental ability, 91
state of crisis in, 44
teaching use of information, 196
Science, as vehicle for teaching relativity of truth, 160
Scientific method, 196
Sears, R. R., 154
Security, vs. independence, 38
Sedentariness, and disease, 170-71
Seeley, John, 44
Self-doubt
of eggheads, 17-18
and inner reality testing, 58

223

Date Due

OCT 2 '78